KENNY'S CAJUN CREOLE COOKBOOK

Hi! Handsome hunting man
Fire your little gun
Bang! Now the little animal
Is dead and dumb and done
Nevermore to peep again, creep again, leap again
Eat or sleep or drink again, Oh what fun!

Walter de la Mare

Cautiously it returned. It met no resistance. It slithered through the
folds of saltmeat and peach. It pressed the seaweed trigger.

Tom Robbins

KENNY'S CAJUN
CREOLE COOKBOOK

Kenny Miller

PRION

First published in Great Britain in 1996 by PRION
32-34 Gordon House Road,
London NW5 1LP

A catalogue record of this book can be obtained
from the British Library

ISBN 1-85375-212-6

Cover and text artwork by Phillip Morrison

Text design by Kelly Flynn

Typeset in Journal by York House Typographic, London
Printed and bound in Italy

Many thanks to:

My Mother for reminding me how to pluck a chicken and equally for ensuring Bill at the Robin Hood, Ironbridge, never missed my cheap ribaldry.

My Father for telling me 'that' should not be in a book read by a market comprising 75% ladies.

My brother Clark, for hating fishing thus leaving all Grandpa's flies to me. To his wife Sue, for letting him come out to play.

My buddies Liz and Tony and all the other personalities who worked for me at KENNY'S. It was particularly Liz's loathing of my incessant, felicitous litany of dishes which kept me cooking and creating, whilst Tony's esoteric advice kept me from wandering through the restaurants in Rabelaisian mode every night.

My Editor Andrew. Who shares with me a 'no bullshit' passion for Huevos Rancheros.

And finally I would like to thank Suzon, for inspiring my decision to travel the two-lane blacktop to Nirvana every night. In search of the unexplored self.

Remember – LOVE IS LIKE A CHEF FROM HELL.
To: Rachel Carson – she sounded the tocsins on man fouling his environment.

To: Paul Durrant

CONTENTS

The Basics

Gumbo, Jambalaya and More

Seafood

CONTENTS

Chicken and Friends

Steak and other Games

Salads

Brunch

Dessert

Lagniappe

THE BASICS

Louisiana

Well, before we really start, I had better bring in my surrogate home of Louisiana.

In 1803, as part of a transaction known as the Louisiana Purchase, Napoleon sold the Americans 800,000 square miles of land for $11.25 million. Louisiana, that part of the purchase which was south of the 33rd parallel, became the 18th state of the Union nine years later.

The area around New Orleans had already experienced a rather lively history; just like any other large port. The first Europeans had reached the area in 1682 with a French guy called La Salle. He settled it for France with the help of thousands of Germans. In 1762, Louis IV gave the area to Spain. The Spanish hated the region as much as the French – hot and troublesome. Just like today really.

In the 1780's the Acadians started to arrive from Nova Scotia, the guys later to be called Cajuns. They could deal with the Catholic Spaniards, although being a little rough around the edges, they colonized out of town - mainly the bayou (swamp) area south of Lafayette.

In the years 1788 and 1794, two great fires decimated the burgeoning city of New Orleans. It had to be rebuilt, hence the prevalence of European architecture, particularly in the French Quarter, with its two-story brick buildings with their elegant wrought-iron railings and balconies, built around a courtyard. The city was now under a fairly relaxed rule, and all sorts of folk entered and stayed in the port and environs – French, Blacks, Scottish, Chinese, Canary Islanders and Santa Dominicans. It was this last bunch who brought in the mulattos and introduced Voodoo to the region. However, back in the jungle or rather France, Napoleon was still in power. Being the spoilt brat he was, he thought he wanted Louisiana back. 'It's my ball.' But he soon decided he did not like it after all, 'all sunshine, no snow.' So he soon exchanged it for a handful of greenbacks.

There was a slight blip in Louisiana's historical progression due to the Civil War, around 1862. Toward the end of the century, the economy gradually began to boom again, heralding the so-called 'The Gilded Age.' One little point, at this time, was the immigration of many Sicilians who are the reason for the big Italian influence in Louisiana Creole cooking.

So you see it was bit of a melting pot. Consequently, the city of New Orleans and the State of Louisiana mean many various things to different peoples. Not definitively American or even Southern. Check out Mardi Gras for a further look into this point.

Louisiana today is a relatively poor State. But the people are proud folk and have the utmost respect for their heritage which is all around - wherever you travel. The State has also the best eating available in the U.S. and some of the best entertainment and exciting living. Not to mention some of the friendliest people. Just do not go to Algiers, which faces New Orleans across the Mississippi, or become lost in the bayous. To be a little more specific however, I want to briefly tell you about the Cajuns.

The Cajuns, from the name 'Acadians', were French settlers, peasants who had left France to seek a new life in Acadia, as Nova Scotia was then called. But they were loyal to France and the Roman Catholic religion. When the British beat them up (for some reason the Brits wanted Nova Scotia too) the Acadians were given two options – pledge allegiance to the Protestant British Crown or 'get outta here!' They left.

Henry W. Longfellow, despite a few historical inaccuracies, honors this debacle in his famous poem 'Evangeline.' The Acadians went all over the place, back to France, to the Caribbean, other parts of Canada but mainly, on hearing of the French settlements around the Mississippi Delta, to Louisiana.

Cajun food in the home and in the neighborhood restaurants of southern Louisiana is based on remarkably few ingredients. It is, however, enlivened with various seasonings and rich cooking styles. The countryside is swampy and the climate sub-tropical, so it does not lend itself to growing crops or rearing cattle. As a result, the Cajuns historically ate whatever they could catch.

Today obviously, life is a little easier, particularly with the money the gas and oil companies bring in. But we should never forget that Cajun food is humble food, the food of the poor and honest, whilst Creole cooking is that of city folk. 'Creole' is from the Spanish 'Criollo,' and was a term bestowed upon New Orleans folk of European descent. It represents many people with varied backgrounds and influences.

But when you mix Cajun and Creole together, watch out!

My Friend the Chile

The chile is one of my favorite subjects, but with over 150 basic varieties knocking around it is rather hard to summarize. If you find chiles as interesting as I do, then I suggest checking out Mark Miller's books on the subject published by Ten Speed Press. He covers all the points in greater detail than I ever could.

However, here are one or two salient points, learnt over many years — often when I failed to treat chiles with the respect they deserved. The spelling 'Chile' generally refers to the plant and the fruit. 'Chili' refers to a dish containing meats and chiles, such as Chili con Carne ('with meat'); 'Chilli' is the powder mix sold commercially.

The capsaicin content, the alkaloid which gives the chile its heat, is measured by the Scoville Scale. Bell peppers register zero, jalapeños (Hal-a-PAY-nyos) register around 5 and the killer habaneros a 10.

The capsaicin is also the reason why we enjoy chiles. It triggers the release of endorphins, which give us that after-dinner glow. This is done by confusing the brain and fooling it into blocking the nerve endings. Similar to stubbing your toe, but without the actual pain.

Always de-seed and de-vein the peppers before use, the seeds and inner fibers are the hottest part. The heel of the knife is best for doing this necessary scraping. Chop them skin downward, this way you lose less juice and run less risk of the knife 'bouncing' and cutting you. Do not pick your nose, rub your eye, or go to the toilet after handling peppers, unless you wear gloves. If you wear gloves you are not my type of cook. Store them loosely in the fridge and never prepare too many, they spoil real fast when cut. Redder and smaller chiles are usually sweeter, hotter and fruitier than green ones. Scotch Bonnets are my favorite, a type of chile habanero found in most West Indian markets. They are the shape of a Scottish tam o'shanter and vary in color from pale yellow, through green, to bright red.

Acadiana, Louisiana, is where most American hot peppers come from. It is the home of Tabasco, Trappey's, Crystal, and hordes of other fiery hot sauces and peppery products. Everywhere you look different kinds of peppers grow, green and red Tabasco chiles, bird's eye, Bahamians, jalapeños, torridos, cayenne, serranos, and Anaheim chiles. The folk down there love them.

The best known hot sauce is Tabasco, made at Avery Island, New Iberia. I personally prefer Louisiana Hot Sauce for general consumption. It is not as spicy or acidic as Tabasco. However, the Avery Island product is hugely popular and now virtually synonymous with hot sauce.

Hot sauce is made from peppers, salt, and vinegar. Fresh peppers are mashed with salt and left for a few years. Then a top grade, distilled vinegar is added, stirred, strained and – voilà! As simple as making wine. But the key to a successful product is the growing of the peppers; the Tabasco pepper is religiously cared for.

The history of Tabasco is much more interesting than its preparation. Before the hot sauce, Avery Island primarily produced salt, as it is a salt mountain surrounded by marshland. It is 30,000 feet high and one and half miles in circumference and was first settled in 1818.

In 1859 a daughter of the Avery family married a guy called McIlhenney, a keen gourmet, traveler, and plant collector. One such plant was an obscure Mexican chile given to him by a traveling Confederate soldier. For a period during the Civil War the Union troops captured New Orleans and Avery Island. They needed the salt for their traveling armies, for meat preservation. In 1865, when the war was over, the Averys returned from their safe Texas haven, to find their family home in ruins. The only surviving plant was the little red pepper. Apparently, McIlhenney played around with the peppers, as you do, and produced a mash to which he added salt – what else? – and vinegar. He soon forgot about it. Three years later he stumbled across the mix and played around again. Out came a hot sauce.

The first sales of 350 perfume bottles full of the mixture were made in 1868. In 1870, McIlhenney patented Tabasco, and the same year he opened an office in London. Today the sauce is so well known it is listed in the dictionary. Not surprising, when you consider that the company ships about 50 million 2-oz bottles to over 100 countries annually.

I still prefer Louisiana Hot Sauce.

You can make hot sauce fairly easily, but it will not compare in style to store-bought products - they are fermented. Nonetheless the homemade variety works just fine. Here is a basic recipe.

Kenny's Hot Sauce

5 large tomatoes, cored
1 small green jalapeño, diced
3 medium red jalapeños, diced
2 cloves garlic, finely chopped

2 tsp cilantro (coriander), coarsely chopped
1 tsp garlic salt
1 tsp coarse black pepper, freshly ground
1 tbl red wine vinegar

Blend together for 2 minutes. Sauté for five minutes, cool and seal.

Seasonings

I aim to have you cooking in two fundamental styles, long and short. Long cooking will have you using pre-mixed spices and short means throwing individual seasonings in the pot as you cook fast. For pre-mixed seasonings, I will give you my favorite three styles. Added to these are mixes for blackening and bronzing.

Seasonings, you have to appreciate, will change in flavor, the more or the less you cook them. This may sound like common sense but I do not think folk treat the seasonings of a dish as real ingredients. They can change just like everything else. Make sense? No? Well I warned you. For example, take big dishes such as gumbo. Here I would ask you to follow one golden rule: use your seasoning mix at three times. Add one third at the beginning, one third at the height of cooking and the last third when the heat has been turned off. The dish will carry on cooking, think of how many times your scrambled eggs have attempted to scramble off into 'rubberdom.' Each dish will require different seasonings, obviously, but with little pertinent extras along the way. The basic principles stay the same. Also, if you choose to use fresh herbs, if you can find them fresh, the textures as well as flavors will change. The purpose of all this is to layer your flavors. Your mouth will recognize red pepper but it will also realize that it is being offered different levels of taste.

The primary seasonings I use are salts of garlic, celery, and onion, the peppers (black, white and red) and herbs ('erbs, as they say). My favorite herbs are thyme, bay, and oregano. I reckon thyme is my favorite, not because Dionysus used it at his parties, but because it used to grow wild behind my favorite fishing hole when I was a kid. I personally loathe tarragon and basil. Even though tarragon has been extolled for years and years for its ability to replace salt in our diet. But what do you care? Use them if you want too, just don't invite me over for dinner. Thanks.

The quality of seasonings can vary immensely. Do not use them if they were in the apartment when you moved in. Please buy new ones. You will appreciate it.

Also remember a pestle and mortar are invaluable at times, for waking up herbs or for mingling flavors in vinaigrettes and dressings. I suggest you make large batches of the seasonings, this way you will find it easier to prepare my dishes. No digging around in the pantry for the elusive onion salt. Similarly, it is wise to label your mixes.

Cajun Seasoning

3 tbl garlic salt
2 tbl onion salt
1 tbl garlic powder
3 tbl cayenne
3 tbl paprika

1 tbl ground white pepper
1 tbl coarse black pepper, freshly ground
2 tbl thyme
1 tbl oregano

Three-way Pepper Seasoning

2 tbl ground hot red pepper
2 tbl ground white pepper

2 tbl coarse black pepper, freshly ground

Sauté Seasoning

1 tbl ground white pepper   1 tbl garlic seasoning
1 tbl garlic powder

Bronze Seasoning

4 tbl paprika   1 tbl ground white pepper
1 tbl cayenne   1 tbl oregano

Blackening

5 tbl paprika   2 tbl coarse-ground black pepper
5 tbl thyme   2 tbl garlic salt
2 tbl oregano   1 tbl garlic powder
3 tbl cayenne

Please note, Cajun seasonings are designed to excite your mouth and complement great foods. Despite common perceptions, Cajun seasonings are not dangerously hot.

The Roux – The Soul Essence

Many Creole and Cajun dishes hail from somewhere way back in traditional French cooking. As a consequence the roux is very prevalent.

The name derives from 'roux beurre', meaning reddish-brown butter. We want it this way - dark-colored; most fancy chefs would not. They feel a roux should stay white, and believe for a dark sauce the 'espagnole' is the only one to use. However, they miss out on the subtleties and mysteries of the colored roux.

It is very important to master the technique for making a roux. Fortunately you do not need to make very large quantities in the home. In my kitchens we called it Cajun Napalm or Agent Roux. It can be dangerous – see below. However, it is a lot safer when made at home, due to the relatively small quantities involved.

The Roux gives many of our Cajun dishes their distinctive flavor and texture. Basically, you are cooking equal parts of oil and flour. The mixture is stirred consistently over a high heat until it reaches the desired color, which can range from blonde, to peanut brown, to near-black. The color depends upon the dish: a light to medium-brown roux for dark meats such as game and a dark colored roux for white meats such as pork or seafood. These combinations make for the best results, although I cannot categorically say why this is. Just be careful and let everyone know it is around and make sure it has cooled right down before use. I always use groundnut oil for my roux, as I do for all frying. I never know which flour I use. I presume it is what the Americans call 'all-purpose' – in other words, plain! Some folks say, and I agree, that the best fat to use for a roux base for the beef gravy used in lubricating such delights as meat pies or chicken-fried steak, is hog lard. You may have to forget your healthy living for a while. Just enjoy.

Groundnut oil, peanut oil or monkey nut oil, or whatever you want to call it, is made from a pulse, not a nut at all. It is also sometimes called arachis oil and is an important commodity oil. Peanut oil smokes at 410°F/210°C, has 7% saturated fatty acids, 53% monounsaturated fats and 29% polyunsaturated fats. To most folk, it has very little taste, but I love its subtle flavor. Mostly cultivated in tropical and sub-tropical regions of the world, the peanut is a very important crop in the southern States and so is readily available.

To make your roux, warm up half a cup (4 fl oz/125 ml) of oil and slowly stir in half a cup (2½ oz/60 g) of flour. Keep the heat high and keep stirring, the oil is becoming hot so take care. The roux will stick, so you have to scrape the bottom of the pan continually, patience is now needed. After 10-15 minutes, or as soon as it has reached the desired color, take the roux off the heat and keep stirring until it has cooled. If you have scorched it, you will have to start again. You will know if you have done so by the presence of small black specks. When the roux is ready, keep it in a low, safe place.

Stocks – Fonds de Cuisine

Stocks are very important to the serious cook and vital to the weekend cook. Believe me.

I don't imagine most folk possess a stockpot. If you do, good. However, any large pot will work. Ideally, it will be your tallest pot and the narrowest. This will leave plenty of space for mingling flavors but the narrowness allows only a limited surface for evaporation.

Fish stock (fumet) is a very concentrated type of stock. It is much easier to produce than the other types, but it is very reliant upon you eating quality white fish, nothing farmed. You also have to be the one who does the filleting. As an alternative, you may be lucky and have a proficient, caring, and knowledgeable local fishmonger, a man who can supply you with fish carcasses.

Fumet in French means the strong, pleasant characteristic smell of a particular food. When you make your first fish stock, you will understand why it has this name. (Well, I hope you will.) Fish stock can be made with either red or white wine, but the quality of the wine you choose has to be relatively good. The best fish to use are flatfish and/or white heads (remove the gills) and white bones. No skin should be used. It's important not to use aluminum pots as the wine's acidity will react with it. Remember, if the wine is not good enough to drink it won't be good enough to cook with. But do not go to extremes. Give the poor stuff to your father. Red wine is less acidic than white, thus you will need more of it to give a similar taste to your stock. You may wish to add some garlic or extra herbs.

Fish is high in water and collagen, the gelatinous compound, as well as calcium and phosphorus. The acid in the wine helps fish collagen dissolve fast in the liquid, consequently fish stocks, unlike meat stocks, can be made quickly.

Fish Stock

Sauté one large, diced onion and one half of a diced carrot together in butter in a stockpot. Add one half cup (2½ oz/60 g) of diced mushrooms and 4 lb/1½ kg of fish bones and gill-less heads. After ten minutes add 2 cups (16 fl oz/500 ml) of good(ish) dry white wine and 8 cups (2½ pints/2 litres) of water. Bring to the boil and cover. Add your favorite seasonings and then simmer for 30 minutes. Add a little extra seasoning and turn off the heat. Leave to cool with the lid on.

To make a good brown (beef) stock you will need a whole load of time and extra cash. Even I don't use it all that much. It is certainly worth making, but after your first attempt you will understand what I am saying. Consequently, you will have to use someone else's recipe if you want to make it!

Chicken Stock

Chicken stock on the other hand, is one major essential element in your cooking. I cannot survive without gallons of it knocking around. Keep plenty of extra frozen. The recipe is also simple. One point though, which you must adhere to - chicken stock should not be refrigerated until it has cooled right down, a bacterial thing. This will also give you time to skim off the inevitable grease it will kick off. Sometimes you will make a stock that is so good it is best consumed as a soup in its own right. No problem. Reduce a little more, add a few vegetables, and you have a cheap, easy meal.

You need as much chicken in the way of chicken bones and scraps as you can muster; necks and backs are best. Place them in a roasting tray with a little water and bake until they are dark brown. Remove them from the tray and place them in your stock pot. Pour a little water in the roasting tray and scrape up the juices. Place in the tray as many veggie trimmings as you have, ideally from onions, celery, carrots, and leeks. Roast for 15 minutes then transfer with all the juices from the pan into the stockpot. Roasting intensifies the flavors. Add some garlic, herbs, salt, and pepper to the stockpot, top with water, and simmer for a long time. When finished, taste it, strain, and cool properly.

Veggie Stock

Roast aromatic vegetables, combine with herbs, and salt and pepper, and simmer in water for 45 minutes.

The Trinity

One of the first things you need to know before embarking on Louisiana cooking is The Holy Trinity. It is sacrosanct to our food and consists of equal parts of onion, celery, and bell pepper.

Onion is a member of the lily family. There are lots of vegetables in the onion family, including garlic, leeks, scallions (spring onions), and shallots. My favorite is the Spanish white onion, small, strong, and not yellow. Onions contain vitamin A and C along with potassium, and are apparently helpful in lowering blood pressure and cholesterol levels. I cannot really comment on their ability to upset lycanthropes and vampires, but some, I know, find the smell a little offensive.

The onion is one of the most important ingredients in the cook's pot, and it's a shame they are taken so much for granted. The Egyptians treated them very differently. They worshipped them. The unique form of a sphere within a sphere within a sphere represented some sort of infinity to them.

The second player in the Trinity is celery or celeriac. The Romans thought celery was good for fending off hangovers. I have never tried it. Try and use all of the vegetable, including the leaves. The root, also known as celeriac, actually has the strongest flavor.

We all know the bell pepper. It is not very exciting, unless cooked. The heat value is zero, and to me everything else about them equates to the same, except for its part in the Trinity.

Sauces

The Cajuns do not care for sauces, but the Creoles do. I come in between. Some dishes cry out for a sauce, others can easily be ruined by them. Similarly, long meals need a sensible mix of varying styles of sauces.

The Creoles say there are three Mother sauces – the brown, the white, and the glacé or glaze, and these three are the basis for all the others. One thing for sure though, making sauces is not easy for the inexperienced, to start with at least. But once mastered, sauces can elevate your food presentations to new heights. Obviously your ingredients are important, especially that stock, but the most important element in sauce-making is timing.

Sauces in my kitchen come in basically two fashions, those prepared with loving care over many hours, which are kept warm throughout the table service – as much fun to me as baking, or learning the multiplication tables. The other type of sauce is born from the buzz only foot-weary chefs or cooks experience. The experience of the chips being down, the pressure intense and unremitting, the odds well in favor of mistakes.

Salsa

Take these guys seriously. In 1992, salsa outsold ketchup/catsup for the first time as America's #1 condiment.(Maybe the 40% of Americans who think ketchup is a vegetable discovered the truth!) I doubt if this is true for South Carolina or the UK, however, but I am hopeful that the day is not too far away. Salsas are tasty, healthy, and colorful. Chiles are much more pleasing to the palate and psyche than sugar-based condiments. A simple salsa, in my opinion, is boring. Nonetheless, even a simple one is better than a slimy, squeezy, store-bought product. Anyone for Cheese Whiz?

My own Salsa Fresca or Tomato Salsa

5 medium red jalapeños
1 medium green bell pepper

1 small red onion

Chop all the ingredients fine and small. This goes against my general rules on chopping, where I try and leave as little flavor on the board and tea-towel as possible. So please use a very sharp knife; you will find you cut yourself more easily on a blunt knife, anyway. Remember to de-vein and de-seed the peppers.

½ cup cilantro (coriander) - coarsely chopped
1 tbl lemon juice
1 tsp garlic, minced

1 tsp coarse-ground black pepper
5 large, very ripe tomatoes

Combine the cilantro, lemon juice, garlic, and pepper. Forty-five minutes before serving, core and de-seed the tomatoes. Chop the flesh coarsely and add to other ingredients. Chill a little more than 30 minutes before serving. We chop the tomatoes last as they may leak.

Garnishing

No big deal really. A spiced apple ring out of the can will do. Only joking. But they are popular in the rural South. I only ever use finely chopped, fresh parsley. There should be no sprigs or indeed anything which resembles a plant shape. What I want you to do is produce a 'green flake.' It does take time but it will end up very light, not at all wet. It transforms dishes which just look so flat. It is miraculous. Try it.

The only other suggestion is a nice colorful dish or plate.

Before we finally, finally move on to the juicy products and dishes, it is important to discuss a few of the more general items. These may appear boring, yet their proper preparation is as vital to good cooking as wine is to the party.

Rice

Rice has now blended into virtually every culture. Half the world's population use this semi-aquatic grass as its staple food. It was first cultivated in China around 2800 BC. Today, it is as important to Paella, Jambalaya, and Risotto as it is to egg-fried rice. Strangely, one quarter of the world's production is from the States. Hello Uncle Ben!

Three main types of rice are grown - long, medium, and short grain. There are however, many special varieties, including aromatic, pecan and black rice. Wild rice, also known as black rice, which is native to the U.S., is not a true member of the rice family, though it grows in water and even tastes like a particularly delicious kind of rice.

Regular milled white rice, with its husk and layers of bran removed, is the type most commonly used today. It is nutritious, being high in complete carbohydrates. This is especially true in the United States where the rice is vitamin-enriched to replace nutrients lost in processing - do not rinse American rice before cooking.

Cooking rice is not too difficult, but it is so integral to Cajun-Creole cooking I feel I should mention it. This is my method.

Boil 4 cups (1¾ pints/1 litre) of water with a tablespoon of olive oil and a teaspoon of sea salt. Add 2 cups (1 lb/450 g) of long-grain white rice to the boiling water. Cover and cook for 10 minutes. Drain, and transfer to a baking tray. Fluff up the rice with a fork and place in the oven. Keep the oven low, around 210°F/100°C/gas mark ½. After 10-15 minutes, the rice will be ready. Fluff up again before serving.

Rice can be real dull. But this depends somewhat upon the dish it is to be served with. There are many ways to 'funk up' the rice and I will leave you to explore the options. 'Red Rice', a specialty of Georgia, is rice cooked with small amounts of green peppers, onions, bacon, and tomato sauce. I like to add color with parsley or diced red jalapeños and flavor by using chicken stock, finely chopped garlic, or soy sauce. It's your ball, play with it.

Pasta

The Chinese claim to have been the first to use pasta but so do the Italians. I don't really care - let them fight over it, is what I say. Durum wheat is the primary ingredient in pasta; its high gluten content produces a tough and elastic dough. The wheat undergoes a series of grindings and siftings as the miller searches out the semolina, ending up with a coarse-ground flour, like cornmeal. To make commercial pasta, the semolina is mixed with water, B-vitamins, and iron. At this stage, any flavorings will be added. These include eggs, herbs, and vegetable purées. You have seen them. Real trendy, although I don't recommend squid ink pasta, unless you enjoy colorful shocks the next morning. I thought I had contracted some dreadful deep, tropical-African disease!

Of course pasta comes in many shapes and sizes, around 600 at the last count. Just have fun with them. Cooking pasta is much easier than cooking rice, and that is not difficult either. Just do not overcook it and consider adding other flavors to the pot.

You don't always need to serve the pasta in a sauce. It is sometimes neat to serve it alongside. Use different presentations and different garnishes. Tossing the cooked pasta in raw egg yolk will make it easier to handle.

Blackening

The night I opened the original Kenny's I had a row with a lawyer from New York City. He said my food was not authentic since I had no 'Blackened dishes' on the menu. He had completely missed the point. My food was authentic BECAUSE I did no Blackening.

The style of cooking called 'Blackening' originated in the kitchens of Chef Paul Prudhomme in 1980. In this style, you coat fish or meat in herbs and spices, then sear it in a white-hot skillet. This seals the outer crust, allowing the juices to remain all on the inside. It produces billows of smoke and should only be attempted outdoors or in a kitchen with a powerful extractor fan. Heating a skillet to the necessary temperatures may not be safe at home – particularly in a busy household. It is possible to achieve similar results by being careful, but I still wouldn't recommend trying it.

Besides, Blackening is not true traditional Cajun-Creole cooking, even if Paul's pedigree allows it to be called Louisiana cooking.

A Note on Servings

I don't feel it is worthwhile for me to pretend that a serving for four of my friends, will be sufficient for four of yours, or vice versa.

Nonetheless I have been bullied into giving you guidelines as to how many folk each recipe will serve – approximately.

But I have to say I never wanted to be presumptuous or didactic.

How do I know what you had for lunch? How do I know the size of your soup bowls? How can I be guilty for not appreciating Gerald still has a hangover?

So, unless otherwise stated the recipes will serve around six folk.

A Note on Measurements

The cup measurement I use throughout is American. Over there they measure lots of ingredients in cups and I find it a quick and easy method compared with all that weighing and measuring. Although I always give metric and imperial alternatives, the cup is an integral part of my style of cooking, and one I hope you will adopt. You can find more information about cup measurements in the glossary at the back of the book.

GUMBO, JAMBALAYA AND MORE

Gumbo

Gumbo is a one-dish meal which sticks to your ribs. A nourishing and filling stew, it's difficult to describe to the uninitiated. The word gumbo has two possible derivations from either of its alternative principle ingredients: filé and okra.

The Natchez and Choctaw Indians of the bayous taught the Cajun settlers many tricks to ensure survival in the swamps. One was the use of sassafras, an aromatic tree of the Laurel family, which they call 'kombo.' They used the bark of the root as a flavoring for root beer – it is horrid! Thankfully, they also used the leaves, pounding them to make 'filé' powder, a basic seasoning in some gumbos. Some folk however, feel the name comes from the word for okra, 'ngombo,' meaning 'ladies finger' in Bantu, the language of many of the slaves. I'll let you choose the derivation.

All my gumbos use okra rather than filé powder. If you can find filé add it to the gumbo just before serving, never earlier. It adds extra thickness and flavor. Also, offer it to your guests at the dinner table.

When you start out to cook gumbo you have to think primordial ooze, Mississippi mud-style and simultaneously think happiness. If you want a decent gumbo you really have to cook it yourself. Restaurant gumbos, except in Louisiana, just do not compare. Believe me.

Gumbo Ya Ya

½ cup (4 fl oz/125 ml) oil, ½ cup (2½ oz/60 g)
plain flour, for the roux
Chicken stock (store-bought is not a crime)
1 cup (8 fl oz/250 ml) Cajun seasoning
1 small ham hock
1 x 2-2½ lb/1 kg chicken
1 or 2 andouille or chorizo sausages
2 cloves garlic, finely chopped
1 cup (5 oz/125 g) okra, chopped

white rice for serving and finely chopped parsley
for garnish

FOR THE TRINITY

1 cup (5 oz/125 g) green bell pepper, coarsely
chopped
1 cup (5 oz/125 g) celery, coarsely chopped
1 cup (5 oz/125 g) white onion, coarsely
chopped

SERVES 6-8

First make your roux as described earlier (see p. 21) and set it aside. Heat the stock. Once the stock is boiling, add the trinity, a third of seasoning and ham hock. Cut the bird into tenths (see p. 238). Slice the andouille thickly and grill it to enable it to lose some of its grease. This is beneficial, as it gives you a free by-product with which to brown the chicken, besides the sausage contributes better if browned.

Simmer the stock for 30 minutes, covered, then add the sausage and the roux. Stir in the roux thoroughly, and once it has disappeared into the stock, add the chicken, as we do not want any of the roux sticking to the chicken meat. After another 30 to 45 minutes, take out the ham hock and scrape off the meat. Coarsely chop it and return to the pot, along with the bone. Check the seasoning and add the second third of it, then wait another 30 minutes or so. The gumbo should by now be thickening. Lower the heat and add the garlic and okra. Taste properly. ('Never trust a skinny chef.') Notice the changes?

Go grab a beer and relax for an hour. Then turn off heat, give a good stir, and add last third of seasoning. Cool properly or serve immediately. Sometimes I feel it tastes better the next day, sometimes I don't really care or can't tell. If the gumbo is kicking off a head of grease, don't worry. Ladle off the top few inches into a tall vestibule (great word) and allow to settle. The grease will kick off again but will be easier to remove.

Serve with white rice and garnish with chopped parsley.

So there is your gumbo. Like real music – jazz and blues – it has overtones of the mysterious, of voodoo and of the all powerful Shaman. It is a one-dish meal. I do not know how it really works, but when it does you can't beat it. The best way to start any cookbook.

Seafood Gumbo

Take this one slow and be confident.

Olive oil
2 pints/1.2 litres fish fumet
2 tbl Cajun seasoning
2 cloves garlic, finely chopped
½ cup (4 fl oz/125 ml) peanut oil and ½ cup
   (2½ oz/60 g) plain flour for the roux
2 cups (10 oz/250 g) firm-textured white fish
2 cups (10 oz/250 g) raw, peeled shrimp or
   prawns

2 cups (10 oz/250 g) mixed seafood (oysters,
   crab, mussels, crawfish, etc.)
Other options are tomatoes, okra, or clamato juice.

FOR THE TRINITY

1 cup (5 oz/125 g) green bell pepper, coarsely
   chopped
1 cup (5 oz/125 g) celery, coarsely chopped
1 cup (5 oz/125 g) white onion, coarsely chopped

SERVES 6-8

Prepare a blonde roux. Sauté the trinity in olive oil until the onion is soft. Add garlic and all the fish and seafood. Cook briefly, then remove from the heat and cover. Bring the stock to boil, add the roux and 1 tbl of seasoning. After one hour or when the stock is thick, take it off the heat. Wait 5 minutes then stir in the rest of the Cajun seasoning, the seafood and trinity. Cover and cook for 10-15 minutes. Then serve over white rice.

Garnishing with cooked, unpeeled prawns, or shredded crabmeat can be fun.

Gumbo Z'herbes

 Gumbo for Lent

2 lb/1 kg Pot greens – kale, mustard, turnip
  greens, shredded cabbage, etc.
6 tbl (3 oz/75 g) butter
3 cloves garlic, finely chopped
3 small green jalapeños, de-seeded and de-veined
1 tbl Worcestershire Sauce
2 cups (10 oz/250 g) trinity
3 cups (1 lb/450 g) white potatoes, cooked and
  diced

3 pints/1.8 litres veggie stock or water
½ cup (4 fl oz/125 ml) blonde roux
2 tbl Cajun seasoning
1 tbl hot sauce
1 tbl soy sauce
3 bay leaves
1 tbl parsley, finely chopped

SERVES 6-8

Many folk add ham hocks and sliced sausage to this gumbo, but I feel that kinda defeats its intrinsic honor. But who am I to comment? Gumbo Z'herbes is usually made with lots of garlic (use elephant garlic if you can find it).

Coarsely chop your greens and sauté in butter, with garlic, jalapeños, and Worcestershire sauce for 10-15 minutes. Bring a pot of stock to the boil and add the roux. After 10 minutes, add 1 tbl of seasoning.

Turn off the heat and add the greens, potatoes, soy and hot sauce to the stock. Cover and leave for 20-30 minutes. Twenty minutes before serving, bring to a simmer and add parsley, the rest of the seasoning, and the bay leaves.

Serve with fresh yeasty rolls.

These are my favorite three gumbos, but as you will see with jambalaya anything goes. There are as many gumbos as there are cooks. Just remember, what ever gumbo you choose to make, always take time over the roux and layer the seasonings. Enjoy.

Red Beans 'n' Rice

The legendary Satchmo, Louis Armstrong, used to sign off his letters with;

> 'red beans 'n' ricely yours,
>   Louis.'

Mondays in New Orleans used to be washday, and in a fashion, they probably still are. The reason why most households would prepare red beans on a Monday is that there was no time to cook after the weekend, especially with all the mess to clear up after having the family and weekend guests around. Consequently a dish was made that requires little, if any attention. I also like the idea of a dish which allows me to go and dream or drink, or both.

Red Beans 'n' Rice is a most wonderful, life-enriching, one-pot meal. Serve it with grilled andouille sausage and buttered cornbread. Garnish with chopped scallions. There are few things better. Trust me.

1 lb/450 g red kidney beans (soaked overnight in cold water, boiled in fresh water for 20 minutes and then drained. This removes the offensive starch)

About 4 cups (32 fl oz/1 litre) chicken stock, enough to cover the beans well and keep topping up

1 medium ham hock (I leave the skin on, you may prefer to discard it)

1-2 andouille sausages or similar, e.g. chorizo, sliced

3 bay leaves
3 garlic gloves, whole
1 tbl garlic salt
1 tbl cayenne

FOR THE TRINITY

1 cup (5 oz/125 g) green bell pepper, coarsely chopped
1 cup (5 oz/125 g) celery, coarsely chopped
1 cup (5 oz/125 g) white onion, coarsely chopped

SERVES 6-8 AS A MAIN DISH, 8-10 AS A SIDE ORDER

Put the beans into a heavy-based pot. Add enough chicken stock to cover. Bring to the boil. Add the rest of the ingredients and bring to the boil. Cover, and cook slowly on very low heat for five hours.

I find it best to remove half the beans after a few hours of cooking, when they are soft, and purée or mash them, then return them to the pot. This will give the dish a creamy texture without losing any of the flavor. When the hock is cooked, scrape the meat off the bone and return both to the pot. At this point check the seasonings. We do not layer the seasonings here because the bean flavor is the prime factor.

Before you start the recipe you may want to steal some of the plain cooked beans for a salad. Simply toss them with cooked shrimp and dressed greens and you are away. It looks great too.

Another idea is to steal a little ham from the hock and make ham croutons or ham butter.

To make ham croutons, process the ham in a blender with fresh garlic and olive oil. Pulse for 3 minutes maximum. Spread on baguette slices, grill for a few minutes, and serve with soup or as required.

For ham butter, shred the ham very finely and mix with coarsely ground black pepper and finely chopped parsley. Maybe add a little grated white onion. Soften a pat of butter and beat it into the ham mixture until thoroughly combined. Place in serving dishes and chill before use.

Cornbread

One item everyone agrees about – cornbread should be served with red beans. That goes for almost all Southern food.

Cornbread is a specialty of the Southern States. One of my favorite restaurants is in Key West, at the southernmost tip of Florida. It is called 'Savannah', and every diner is greeted at the table with an iron skillet (frying pan) of oven-fresh cornbread. When 'Chez Helene' in New Orleans was open, the basket of various breads they would place on every table always included air-light corn muffins.

Cornbread is easy and fast, you will be a fool not to give it a go. Besides, how many folk do you know who cook cornbread at home? (Please don't use 'Aunt Jemima' or any other packet mix.)

1½ cups (8 oz/200 g) coarse yellow cornmeal
½ cup (2½ oz/60 g) plain flour
2 tsp baking powder
1 tsp salt
2 tsp white sugar

1 medium onion, grated
1 tbl olive oil
1 egg, beaten
1½ cups (12 fl oz/375 ml) milk

Real easy. Sift dry ingredients together with onion. Mix oil, egg, and milk, until smooth. Combine with dry ingredients. Bake at 425°F/220°C/gas mark 7, for 20 minutes or until golden-brown. Check with a skewer, which should come out clean when the cornbread is ready.

Other ingredients I have used to make cornbread funky are: crackling, crumbled fried bacon, molasses, diced jalapeños, roasted corn kernels, cheese, and garlic.

Turtle Black Bean Soup

After red beans come black beans. Black Bean Soup is of Cuban, via Spanish, origin. It is the official soup of Florida and is consumed in vast quantities, everywhere from the finest restaurants to the most humble lodgings.

Its defining characteristic is a sofrito, aromatic vegetables braised in oil, often with salt pork. The sofrito is to Hispanic dishes what the trinity and the roux are to Cajun cooking. The slow sauté of onions, bell peppers and garlic in fat, extracts maximum flavor, giving soul to the beans. The beans are frijoles negros, also known as 'turtle beans,' the cornerstone of

Hispanic cooking. They are small, black and kidney shaped with a tiny white eye and a mild, earthy flavor.

First point, when making Turtle Black Bean Soup, always use a wooden spoon, metallic spoons can leave a little of their metallic taste.

1 thick slice of pork belly, coarsely chopped
1 tbl olive oil
3 cloves garlic
1 tbl red wine vinegar
2 tsp garlic salt
2 tsp celery salt
2 tsp paprika
2 tsp cayenne
2 tsp cumin
4 bay leaves
2 tsp coarse-ground black pepper
3 pints/1.8 litres chicken stock

1 lb/450 g black beans, soaked in cold water
  overnight, and drained
1 small ham hock, parboiled in unsalted water
  for 45 minutes
1 or more red and green jalapeños diced
1 cup (8 fl oz/250 ml) strong red wine

FOR THE TRINITY

1 cup (5 oz/125 g) red bell pepper, coarsely
  chopped
1 cup (5 oz/125 g) celery, coarsely chopped
1 cup (5 oz/125 g) onion, coarsely chopped

SERVES 6-8

Sauté the trinity and chopped pork in oil for ten minutes over a high heat. Add the garlic, vinegar, and half of the seasoning. Stir well, then remove from the heat. We want the flavors to infuse. Heat up the chicken stock to boiling, add the sofrito and beans. Split the ham hock to the bone and loosen the skin, add to the pot with the jalapeños.

After 40 minutes, top with more stock if needed and add the rest of the seasoning. Pull the meat off the ham bone and return with the bone to the pot. Cook for a further 60 minutes then take off heat and leave to rest, following another good stir. Check the seasoning. Add wine and stir again, then serve.

Garnish as you feel is best, just aim for color. Try sour cream ('going to the prom'), diced white onion (soaked in white wine vinegar), finely chopped parsley, diced red jalapeños, and/or a drop or two of sherry. 'Going to the prom' may alleviate the heat for some folk.

The soup is relatively simple to prepare, it should just be allowed to bubble away, alone, pumping its mysteries throughout the house, soothing you along the way with its promises. Trust me it works.

Fried Eggplant with Creole Mustard Dip

Personally I hate eggplant, ever since an encounter with a dubious Moussaka. I first saw fried eggplant at 'Mr B's' in New Orleans where it is a standard dish.

1 medium eggplant (aubergine), peeled and cut into fingers
Batter
2 eggs
½ cup (4 fl oz/125 ml) milk
½ cup (2½ oz/60 g) plain flour

1 cup (5 oz/125 g) plain flour for dredging
2 cups (10 oz/250 g) breadcrumbs, seasoned with cayenne, garlic salt, coarse ground black pepper, and thyme
Oil for deep frying

A STARTER FOR 4

This is another simple but satisfying recipe. But work fast, or the eggplant begins to lose its flavor. Keep one hand for 'dry' and one for 'wet.'

Dip the eggplant in the batter, then in flour, then in batter again, and finally in breadcrumbs. As soon as all eggplant is finished either cover and refrigerate, or fry until golden.

Serve with Creole Mustard Dip.

Creole Mustard Dip

2 tbl Creole or coarse-grained mustard
3 tbl mayonnaise
2 tsp horseradish sauce
1 tsp white wine vinegar

2 tbl olive oil
1 tsp garlic salt
1 tsp coarse-ground black pepper
1 tbl lemon juice

Combine and refrigerate.

Jambalaya

Well here goes, all you Creole cuisinières. This is the best-known dish to originate in Louisiana and it scares me to think I am to write an introduction and recipe. This despite having cooked it thousands of times. I once cooked six hundred jambalayas in three nights at a Cajun Festival. No fuss.

The history of Jambalaya (jahm-buh-LIE-yah), like that of Gumbo, Etouffée, Court bouillon, Hoppin' John and many others is indicative of the complex nature of Southern cooking. Jambalaya has no definitive recipe, but is very special to Louisiana, despite some folk saying it is just an American version of Paella. It is not.

Jambalaya is an empty larder dish – anything goes provided rice, tomatoes and the trinity are included. Jambalaya is traditionally very spicy.

Imagine you owned a Plantation house in the Mississippi basin back in the 1700's. You grew cotton, rice, oranges, coffee, etc. The guys working the fields were slaves of African extraction. These guys had a good appetite, and fortunately so did your family, guests and house servants. To feed the workers out in the fields, you would simply drop scraps from the dinner table, which invariably included ham (jambon/jamba), into a big pot and have it dragged out to the fields. En route, various items which grew wild or semi-wild, were added, such as herbs, tomatoes and rice. The Plantation owners of French extraction, used terms such as 'à la' and 'voilà' and by chance the African slaves called rice 'ya.' Consequently, we have jamba/la/ya.

Creole Sauce

The creole sauce is used as the basis for Jambalaya and many other of the signature dishes. It can be kept in stock so that a Jambalaya can be cooked up quickly.

2 cloves garlic, finely chopped
Olive oil
1 tsp garlic salt
1 tsp white pepper
1 tbl Worcestershire Sauce
1 tbl Louisiana Hot Sauce
1 tbl lemon juice
1³/₄ lb/800 g plum tomatoes, crushed (use your hands)
1 tbl tomato purée
6 fresh bay leaves
1 tbl oregano

1 tbl thyme
2 tsp onion powder
1 tbl cayenne
1 tbl paprika
About 4 cups (1³/₄ pints/1 litre) water

FOR THE TRINITY

1 cup (5 oz/125 g) green bell pepper, coarsely chopped
1 cup (5 oz/125 g) celery, coarsely chopped
1 cup (5 oz/125 g) white onion, coarsely chopped

Sauté trinity and garlic in oil, until onion is soft. Add garlic salt, white pepper and Worcestershire sauce. Cook for five minutes. Add Hot Sauce and lemon juice, then slowly mix in plum tomatoes. Cook for five minutes then blend in the tomato purée, loosen with a cup (8 fl oz/250 ml) of water. Add rest of seasonings. Bring to the boil, reduce the heat and simmer, covered, for 30 minutes. Add 3 cups (1¹/₄ pints/750 ml) water and cook, covered, until thick(ish) about 20 minutes. Remove from heat and keep stirring until cool. Cool completely before storing in the refrigerator.

Po' Man's Jambalaya

This is the original way of serving Jambalaya.

5 cups (2 pints/1.2 litres) Creole sauce
3 andouille or smoked sausages, sliced
1 small green jalapeño, diced
2 cloves garlic, finely chopped
Olive oil
1 cup (10 oz/250 g) smoked ham, chopped
1 tbl Cajun seasoning

3 cups (1¼ pints/750 ml) chicken stock
2 cups (10 oz/250 g) uncooked long grain white
rice
2 cups (10 oz/250 g) cooked roast chicken
2 cups (10 oz/250 g) shrimp, peeled and chopped
3 scallions (spring onions), chopped
1 tbl parsley, finely chopped

SERVES 8-10

Prepare the Creole sauce and keep it warm. Sauté the andouille, garlic, and jalapeño in the oil for five minutes. Add the ham and seasoning, mix well, and remove from the heat.

Heat the chicken stock and add rice. Cook for 5 minutes maximum and add andouille mix. Take off heat and mix in chicken, shrimp, scallions and parsley. Add the Creole sauce. Transfer to a baking dish and place in a pre-heated 375°F/190°C/gas mark 5 oven. Bake for 20 minutes and serve.

House Jambalaya

This is the fancy way of serving jambalaya.

1 medium white onion, diced
2 oz/60 g butter
2 cloves garlic, finely chopped
2 cups (10 oz/250 g) tasso (see p. 49) or other
  ham, finely diced
1 tbl parsley, finely chopped
6 cups (2 ¼ pints/1 ½ litres) chicken stock
1 tsp garlic salt
1 tsp cayenne
1 small red onion, grated

2 cups (1 lb/450 g) long-grain white rice
4 cups (1 ¾ pints/1 litre) Creole sauce (see p. 42)
1 cup (8 fl oz/250 ml) white wine
2 andouille or smoked sausage links, sliced
2 cups (10 oz/250 g) crawfish tails
1 chicken breast, diced small
2 cups (10 oz/250 g) shrimp, diced
1 cup (5 oz/125 g) scallions (spring onions),
  diced
Parsley for garnishing, finely chopped

SERVES 6-8

Sauté the onion in butter until brown. Take off heat and add garlic, tasso, and parsley. Heat chicken stock with garlic salt and cayenne. As it begins to simmer, add red onion and tasso mix. Cook for 10 minutes then add rice, lower heat and cover.

Bring Creole sauce to a simmer with wine. Add the other ingredients, turn off heat and cover.

As soon as rice is cooked, stir well. Then form one or two rice molds on each plate. (Firmly press rice into ramekins or cups and invert on plate). Leave ramekin in place.

Stir Creole sauce mix well, check chicken and shrimp are cooked, and arrange around ramekins. Remove ramekins and garnish with parsley. Enjoy.

Cajun Jambalaya

Baby back ribs, ham bone meat, or small pork chops can be also added to the mix. Roast them first.

4 cloves garlic, finely chopped
5 tbl (2½ oz/60 g) butter
1 cup (8 fl oz/250 ml) chicken stock
2 small red jalapeños, finely diced
2 large tomatoes, cored and chopped
1 tsp garlic salt
1 tsp paprika
1 tsp cayenne
3 andouille or smoked sausages, sliced

2 cups (10 oz/250 g) tasso, finely diced

FOR THE TRINITY

1 cup (5 oz/125 g) green bell pepper, coarsely
  chopped
1 cup (5 oz/125 g) celery, coarsely chopped
1 cup (5 oz/125 g) white onion, coarsely
  chopped

SERVES 6-8

Sauté trinity and garlic in butter until onion is soft. Moisten with chicken stock. Add other ingredients and cook for 10 minutes. Remove from heat and cover.

2 cups (1 lb/450 g) long-grain white rice,
  parboiled
1 tbl parsley, finely chopped
1 cup (5 oz/125 g) scallions (spring onions),
  diced

2 cups (10 oz/250 g) cooked, boned, skinless
  poultry meat (preferably quail, although
  chicken will do), finely chopped
1 tsp garlic salt
1 tsp black pepper, freshly ground

Combine all ingredients in a baking dish, mix well, cover with chicken stock. Bake at 325°F/170°C/gas mark 3, until rice is cooked, about 30 minutes.

Take from oven and heat trinity sauce. Mix well, then serve in bowls.

Sauce Piquante

Sauce piquante is my own Creole sauce made with a roux and chicken stock; fresh tomatoes are the preference this time. Like other sauces, it has a variety of applications, as well as being a dish in its own right.

1 x 2-3lb (1 kg) chicken cut into tenths, or
    smaller
About 2 cups (10 oz/250 g) plain flour
1 cup (8 fl oz/250 ml) olive oil
1 tbl dark roux
1 cup (8 fl oz/250 ml) red wine
1 tbl Cajun seasoning
About 4 cups (1³/₄ pints/
    1 litre) chicken stock
5 large tomatoes, cored and diced
3 scallions (spring onions), diced

1 tbl Louisiana Hot Sauce
2 small red jalapeños, finely diced
Parsley, finely chopped and scallions (spring
    onions) for garnish

FOR THE TRINITY

1 cup (5 oz/125 g) green bell pepper, coarsely
    chopped
1 cup (5 oz/125 g) celery, coarsely chopped
1 cup (5 oz/125 g) white onion, coarsely
    chopped

SERVES 4-6

Dredge the chicken pieces in flour then thoroughly brown them in oil.

Remove the chicken and add the roux to pan. As soon as the roux has heated, add trinity and Cajun seasoning. Cook for 5 minutes then add enough chicken stock to make twice the amount of liquid. Stir well. Bring to the boil then reduce the heat, so the mixture simmers. Add the tomatoes, scallions and Louisiana Hot Sauce and mix in then a little more chicken stock. Cook for twenty minutes. Add jalapeños and chicken, half cover with stock, and cook until chicken is ready.

Add wine and hot sauce, take off heat and cover.

White rice is de rigeur when Sauce Piquante is served as a dish in its own right, but not the only accompaniment we can use; noodles or mashed potatoes are fine.

Arrange the rice on a plate, stir the chicken mixture well and spoon it over the rice. Garnish with parsley and chopped scallions.

Mock Turtle Soup

I cooked turtle once, I think. At least, I was told it was turtle meat, but on reflection, it could have been armadillo or even duck-billed platypus, for all I knew. Especially when I read that Darwin said armadillo tastes like duck. The meat was pinkish-gray, stringy, and tough. The effort was made anyway. It did not sell. Nonetheless I loved the recipe, sherry, tomatoes, and wine, plus a roux. It sounded great. Consequently, I produced a mock version, using a more acceptable meat. Traditionally, mock versions use a calf's head, but I used ground pork. The result, in my opinion — tremendous! It still failed to sell.

5 tbl (2½ oz/60 g) butter or oil
1 tbl garlic, finely chopped
5 oz/125 g smoked pork, finely diced
10 oz/250 g fresh, lean pork, finely chopped
1 tsp nutmeg
1 tsp mace
3 pints/1.8 litres chicken stock
1 cup (8 fl oz/250 ml) medium roux
3 cups (1 lb/450 g) chopped plum tomatoes
2 tbl tomato purée
2 tbl Cajun seasoning
½ cup (4 fl oz/125 ml) dark, sweet sherry

½ cup (4 fl oz/125 ml) red wine
1 tbl Worcestershire Sauce
2 hard-boiled eggs, chopped
2½ oz/60 g parsley, finely chopped

FOR THE TRINITY

1 cup (5 oz/125 g) green bell pepper, coarsely chopped
1 cup (5 oz/125 g) celery, coarsely chopped
1 cup (5 oz/125 g) white onion, coarsely chopped

SERVES 6-8

Sauté trinity in butter or oil until onion is translucent. Add garlic and smoked pork. Cook for five minutes. Use a slotted spoon to remove all and brown the finely diced fresh pork in the residual oils. Once browned, add nutmeg and mace. Cook for 5 minutes. Moisten with a little stock. In a large pot, bring the stock to the boil add roux, tomatoes and tomato purée. Cook for twenty minutes then add half of seasoning and both meat mixtures. Cook for twenty minutes. Add rest of seasoning, sherry, wine and Worcestershire Sauce. Reduce until thick. Taste. Garnish with the hard boiled eggs and chopped parsley.

Oyster Stews

'There is nothing in Christianity or Buddhism that quite matches
the sympathetic unselfishness of an oyster'

Saki

Both the following soups are glorious, gourmet soups, New Orleans style.
I seldom enjoy cooked oysters. It does not really matter which type of
oyster you use. Just make sure they are fresh and that you retain the liquid.
Only ever cook oysters until the edges begin to curl — they are 80% water.

I use canned artichokes, fresh are a pain in the ass. Once at dinner, not
knowing how to eat the infernal things, I hid the leaves in my pockets. I
can only think everyone else did the same.

Creamed Oyster Stew

5 tbl (2½ oz/60 g) butter
1 cup (8 fl oz/250 ml) fish stock
24 oysters with their liquid
1 cup (5 oz/125 g) white potatoes, parboiled and
   cut into small cubes
Salt and pepper
1 cup (8 fl oz/250 ml) white wine
1 cup (8 fl oz/250 ml) double cream
2 tsp garlic salt

1 tsp cayenne
Paprika for garnishing

FOR THE TRINITY

1 cup (5 oz/125 g) green bell pepper, finely
   chopped
1 cup (5 oz/125 g) celery, finely chopped
1 cup (5 oz/125 g) white onion, grated

PORTION 4-6 OYSTERS PER BOWL

48

Sauté the trinity in butter until onion is translucent. Separately, bring the stock and oyster liquid to a simmer. Skim off any funny stuff.

Add potatoes to trinity with salt and pepper, cook for 5 minutes. Moisten with 2 tbl of the wine. Add the rest of the wine to the stock, simmer, then strain over potatoes. When simmering again, add cream, garlic salt and cayenne. As soon as it begins to steam again add the oysters. Are you now working fast and beginning to worry? Have a quick slug on the wine. As soon as the edges of the oysters begin to curl turn off heat and serve. Garnish with paprika. Rest. Well done!

Oyster and Artichoke Soup

4-8 artichoke hearts
1 cup (8 fl oz/250 ml) chicken stock
1 tsp thyme
1 tsp white pepper
4 fresh bay leaves
2 cups (16 fl oz/500 ml) seafood or fish stock
5 tbl (2½ oz/60 g) butter
1 large white onion, diced small

5 scallions (spring onions), diced
24 or so oysters, with liquid
1 cup (8 fl oz/250 ml) double cream
1 tbl plain flour
4 rashers streaky bacon, diced and fried crispy
2½ oz/60 g parsley, finely chopped
Smoked oysters as an option for garnish

PORTION 4-6 OYSTERS PER BOWL

Boil artichokes in chicken stock until soft. Remove them and add seasonings and seafood stock to the chicken stock. Bring to the boil. Separately sauté the onion, scallion, and bacon until onion is soft. Remove from heat and add oysters, reserving the liquid. Keep stirring until the pan is cool. Add oyster liquid to the stocks, reduce to a simmer. After 10 minutes, add the cream and sift in flour. The stock should be thick. If not, keep reducing it. Discard the bay leaves.

Divide the oyster mix into individual servings and pour stock over them. Garnish with smoked oysters or paprika and chopped chives. Leave a couple minutes before serving, this will heat up the oysters and allow the smoked oysters to wake up.

Corn and Crab Bisque

Bisque is a rich soup made from shellfish. In Louisiana, the most popular bisque is made from crawfish. However, it is too difficult and costly for me, sitting in London, to reproduce for you here. In the northern United States, lobster bisque is big news, like in France. After cooking, the shells are crushed and strained into the stock.

In Louisiana, the crawfish heads are stuffed with the tail meat and the preparation takes forever. Lots of fuss.

2 cobs fresh sweetcorn, shucked and cleaned
2 scallions (spring onions), chopped
1/2 cup (5 oz/125 g) unsalted butter
1 tsp garlic salt
1 tsp ground white pepper
1/2 tsp thyme
1/2 tsp oregano

2 cups (16 fl oz/500 ml) fish stock
1 cup (8 fl oz/250 ml) white wine
1/4 cup (2 fl oz/60 ml) double cream
1 tbl brandy
10 oz/250 g or more of white crabmeat
Chopped cilantro (coriander) for garnish

SERVES 4

Sauté corn and scallions in butter, until corn begins to brown. Add seasoning and fish stock, bring to simmer, add wine. Check seasoning - I say this as strengths of seasonings vary. Fold in cream and as soon as it begins to bubble, add brandy and remove from heat. Portion the crabmeat into the soup bowls and pour the liquid over it. I suggest you garnish with chopped cilantro.

If you have some shucked corn cobs left over from, say, Macquechoux or Creamed corn prep, boil them up for a stronger stock.

Creole Peanut Soup

Some folk call this Goober Soup, from the Congelese word 'nguba', meaning peanut. I once tried this soup to see if my American customers would go for it. To my surprise they did! But then again Americans eat some 800 million pounds weight of peanut butter each year. Elvis loved peanut butter and banana sandwiches. But despite The King, I cannot abide the stuff. However in true philanthropic fashion, I've included the recipe and if you enjoy peanut butter you'll love this soup. Aim to keep the flavor mild. You may even convince a few non-believers to try it. What's more, it's quick and easy to prepare.

1 white onion, finely chopped
2 tbl (1 oz/25 g) butter
4 cups (1¾ pints/1 litre) chicken or veggie stock
½ tsp ginger
½ tsp nutmeg
½ tsp celery salt

5 oz/125 g crunchy peanut butter
4 fl oz/125 ml double cream
8 fl oz/250 ml white wine
Whole or crushed peanuts and chopped cilantro
  (coriander) for garnish

ONE JAR OF PEANUT BUTTER IS AMPLE FOR 4-6 FOLKS

Sauté white onion in butter until soft. Combine with chicken or veggie stock and the spices. Once it is boiling add peanut butter, crunchy is best I believe. To dilute the strength of the flavor add cream and white wine. You may feel the need to add salt and pepper, it is hard to find a cookbook which does not tell us to, EVERY TIME. Why? You don't need to. Believe me. Garnish with whole or crushed peanuts and maybe coarsely chopped cilantro.

Creole Onion Soup

I have heard this soup called 'Looney Soup.' It is one of the many traditional French dishes adapted by the Creoles of New Orleans. The combination of two stocks added to lightly caramelized onions creates an interesting flavor. Try to find white Spanish onions. Top the soup with garlic bread and loads of Gruyère cheese. To make garlic bread I use a mix of olive oil and crushed garlic, I press it into the bread and bake it with butter. Garlic salt usually finds its way in too.

6 tbl (3 oz/75 g) unsalted butter
6 large white onions, sliced
1 tbl garlic salt
1 tbl white pepper
1 tsp black pepper, freshly ground
1 tbl brown sugar
2½ cups (1 pint/600 ml) beef stock

½ cup (2½ oz/60 g) plain flour
2 pints/1.2 litres chicken stock
2 tsp soy sauce
1 tsp Worcestershire Sauce
6 slices garlic bread
6 tbl grated Gruyère cheese
Parsley, finely chopped

SERVES 4-6

Melt the butter slowly. Don't burn it. Add sliced onion and half the garlic salt, half the white pepper, the black pepper and the sugar. Keep cooking and stirring, for 20 minutes, or until the onions are caramelized, the sugar turning the onions brown and sweet. Add the beef stock, bring to boil, and sift in flour. No lumps please. Add rest of salt and pepper and then chicken stock.

Simmer for around 3-4 hours, keep stirring. Take off heat and mix in soy and Worcestershire sauces. To serve, top each bowl with garlic bread and cheese, then place under a hot grill until cheese is melted, about two minutes.

The bowls will be hot, so be careful and tell your guests. This soup is filling so don't rush the next course. Garnish with the chopped parsley.

Creole Tomato Soup

The beefsteak tomato grows wild in Louisiana, particularly around Big Mamou where the locals pick them when the sun makes their skins burst. I have never tasted a similar tomato, anywhere.

One tip with this soup – blend it when it has cooled down, just in case you fill the blender too high and it begins to fly all around the kitchen. I missed this little point the first time round. Molten tomato broth was spraying everything within a 10-foot radius, especially me. An 'apple of love' volcano. I could not get anywhere near it until it had emptied itself half-way down the bowl. 'Some days just ain't fair' is what I say. Try growing your own tomatoes or at least buy from a local specialty supplier. Vine-ripened are the best. Supermarket tomatoes are pitiful and tasteless, and a waste of good manure.

The soup can be made a little fancy with the addition of a firm fleshed white fish, poached and cut into cubes – just as a garnish maybe. Crème fraîche also works well with chopped chives.

3 tbl olive oil
2 cloves garlic, crushed
1 large yellow onion, diced
1 red bell pepper, diced
1 tbl fresh oregano, chopped
1 tsp sage

1 tsp garlic salt
1 tsp coarse-ground black pepper
6 large ripe tomatoes, quartered
1 tsp soy sauce
4 cups (1¾ pints/1 litre) water
4 tbl garlic croutons (optional)

SERVES 4-6

Heat oil and sauté garlic, onion, and pepper for ten minutes. Remove from heat and mix in the oregano, sage, garlic salt, and black pepper. Cook for five minutes then add water and tomatoes and cook for another five minutes. Check seasoning and add soy sauce. Let cool. Purée in a blender. Re-heat slowly, serve and garnish with garlic croutons, a drop of crème fraîche per diner and/or cubes of poached fish.

Five Onion Soup

There are many types of onion, and various other plants which fit somewhere under the onion banner. My soup plays with the general theme, but is exceptional nonetheless. It comes under my preferred style of 'sautéed' soups, where everything is prepared in advance and the soup quickly compiled.

Spring onions are known as scallions on the East Coast of the United States and green onions in the West. I respect them so much, they are in nearly every recipe.

If you don't know how to clean leeks properly I suggest you put them in the dish-washer on rinse – having slit one side first, of course.

Shallots are a bore to peel, do them first. You may find it less wasteful and easier to cut chives up with scissors, a much under-utilized kitchen utensil.

NO! I don't know of any cure for onion crying. So just get on with it.

Garlic I leave unpeeled in this recipe, it makes the cloves a little milder. An important factor if you have anyone stay over.

1 leek , washed and sliced	1 tsp garlic salt
6 scallions (spring onions), diced (I always include the whites)	1 tsp onion salt
	½ cup (4 fl oz/125 ml) oil
1 medium red onion, sliced	½ cup (2½ oz/60 g) plain flour
3 medium white onions, diced	2 pints/1.2 litres chicken stock
3 shallots, diced (optional)	3 cloves garlic, finely chopped
5 tbl (2½ oz/60 g) unsalted butter	2 tbl parsley, finely chopped
2 tsp white pepper	3 chives, snipped fine

SERVES 4-6

54

Sauté the leeks, scallions, red and white onions and shallots, if using, in the butter. After 5 minutes, add the pepper, garlic salt and onion salt. Cook for a further few minutes. Make a blonde roux from all but one tbl of the oil and flour. Heat the stock and blend in roux, bring to a simmer, add garlic and cooked onion mix, and cook for 10-15 minutes. Meanwhile sauté parsley and chives in the rest of the olive oil. Remove from heat after five minutes, drain, and keep for garnish.

Liquid smoke (see p. 238) and wild mushrooms can be added for variety.

SEAFOOD

Shrimp Creole

Sauce Piquante is the original spicy tomato accompaniment to many Creole dishes. Today, it is a dish in its own right. Shrimp Creole, the most popular version, is common throughout the States and is usually on the menu as an alternative to fried shrimp dishes. Consequently, it has become an ubiquitous, unctuous embarrassment. But prepared properly by you, me, and the folk of Louisiana it is heavenly. Fresh, crunchy and spicy. The tomato broth should be light and uplifting. Shrimp, a collective plural, is used to denote prawns in the U.S.

In general my recipes call for large shrimp. If you only have pre-cooked, pre-peeled, pre-glazed, pre-everything shrimp, then add them right at the end. To gain a little extra richness add red wine and sherry to the stock. Do not be scared by the level of seasoning, the rice will absorb the heat of the spice and besides the excitement will only last for a few minutes. Trust me.

2 tbl (1 oz/25 g) butter
3 tsp Cajun seasoning
2 cups (16 fl oz/500 ml) fish stock
2 tsp sugar
3 scallions (spring onions), chopped
1 medium red jalapeño
6 large tomatoes, cored and coarsely chopped
2 lb/1 kg large shrimp, shelled, un-cooked, de-veined
1 tbl lemon juice

Hot cooked white rice
Finely chopped parsley for garnishing

FOR THE TRINITY

1 cup (5 oz/125 g) green bell pepper, coarsely chopped
1 cup (5 oz/125 g) celery, coarsely chopped
1 cup (5 oz/125 g) white onion, coarsely chopped

SERVES 6-8

Sauté trinity until soft in the butter. Add one third of the seasoning. Mix and cool. Bring the stock to the boil, reduce the heat to a simmer, add sugar, and second third of seasoning. Cook until thick. Add scallions and jalapeños, then trinity mix. Cook until hot, then add tomatoes and shrimp, and the rest of the Cajun seasoning. Cook until shrimp are cooked. Remove from heat. Add lemon juice.

Press the rice into individual molds and unmold one on each plate. Remove shrimp from the pot and arrange over the rice molds, tails upward, head facing down into the rice. Ladle the sauce over the shrimp. Garnish with parsley.

Courtbouillon

'Coo-be-yon' is a genuine Cajun dish, albeit an adaptation from the French, where it refers to an aromatic liquor or stock in which meat or fish are braised.

Make a Sauce Piquante with added red wine, mushrooms, and a stock. Courtbouillon is usually served with a firm-textured white fish like the Red Drum ('Red Fish'), recently endangered, but apparently bouncing back due to a ban on commercial fishing.

2 cups (16 fl oz/500 ml) Creole sauce (see p. 42)
1 cup (8 fl oz/ 250 ml) red wine
½ cup (4 fl oz/125 ml) fish stock
4 white fish fillets, such as snapper or grouper
Garlic salt

Paprika
Coarse-ground black pepper
1 tbl dark roux
1 cup (5 oz/125 g) mushrooms, coarsely chopped

SERVES 4

Mix the Creole sauce, wine, and stock together and bring to boil. Sprinkle the fish with garlic salt, paprika, and coarsely-ground black pepper. Add the roux and stir well. As soon as the roux has blended take down to a simmer and add mushrooms. After five minutes lower in fillets and remove from the heat. Cover with lid and leave for 10-15 minutes.

Prepare platters of white rice and serve a fillet on top of each. Pour your courtbouillon over the top and garnish with chopped fine parsley and diced scallions. Enjoy.

Bronzed Mahi-Mahi with Mango Salsa

...parting day
>Dies like a dolphin, whom each pang imbues
>With a new color, as it gasps away
>The last still loveliest 'till - 't is gone and
>all is gray.

>Lord Byron

This is my favorite fish dish in the book. Mahi-mahi is the Hawaiian name for dolphin fish. It's the most beautiful fish in the sea, whose brilliant colors – yellow – green – turquoise – we rarely see. They mostly fade straight away after being caught. The fish swim in tropical and sub-tropical waters, close to the surface, off the coasts of California, Hawaii, the Gulf of Mexico and the South Atlantic. Daddy Mahi have big square heads and can grow up to 50 lbs (22 kg). The meat is white, tender, sweet and lean. There are no substitutes. Books will tell you different. Go catch them. Sometimes they are called Dorado, but there is another fish which is the real Dorado. You can find Mahi-mahi at good fishmongers, try one serving the Caribbean community.

4 6 oz (175 g) Mahi-mahi fillets, skinned
6 tbl (3 oz/75 g) unsalted butter
1 tsp garlic salt
1 tbl parsley, finely chopped
1 tbl bronze mix (see p. 20)

Juice of 1 lime
1 medium white onion, grated
Mango salsa (see over)
1 lettuce, leaves separated, tossed in Italian
   dressing

SERVES 4

Heat the butter slowly, add garlic salt, parsley, and onion. Sprinkle the fish on one side with bronze mix, place in pan. Cook for 4 minutes. Turn the fish, add the lime juice to pan, and keep shaking it. Cook for a further 3-4 minutes. Remove from pan and serve on warm plates. Add mango salsa and lettuce leaves.

Mango Salsa

I have to admit, at first I was worried about making a gaily-colored salsa. Would people think my food was a bit 'foo-foo'? and I don't mean the Jamaican dish with yams, plantains and cassava. Would they think all my golf shots had parsley on them? But after a food critic derided me for 'Blackened Bluefish with Mango Coulis' I had to make Mango Salsa. This salsa became very popular, not only for its colors, but for its refreshing taste and texture. Who cares if we are a bit 'foo-foo' now and again?

Mango is known as 'the king of fruits' and comes from Africa. When you buy mangoes they should be firm to the touch, but yield slightly. Mango Salsa is fun to make, just make sure you use brown sugar and Balsamic Vinegar.

1 medium-size red bell pepper, de-seeded and
*   finely chopped*
½ cup (2½ oz/60 g) cilantro (coriander), finely
*   chopped*
1 small red onion, finely chopped
3 mangoes, pitted and diced small, reserving the
*   juice*

1 tsp garlic salt
1 tsp coarse-ground black pepper
1 tbl lemon juice
1 tbl Balsamic vinegar
2 tsp brown sugar

Combine all the ingredients and chill the salsa.

You may wish to take this salsa a little further, into the realms of tropicana. Do this by the addition of other fruit such as papaya, blood oranges, tamarillos and maybe mint leaves.

Tamarillos have nothing to do with our Southern cooking, but then again neither does souchong. They are wonderful for decorating plates. Tomarillos are the 'tree tomato' of the Antipodes, particularly New Zealand. In a way, kiwi fruit with street cred. Slice them finely, and cover with a good olive oil and a dash of vinegar. Leave in the dark for a few hours and behold! (I discovered them when the veg. guy misunderstood my request for 'tomatillos.')

Seafood Mamou

Mamou is in Southern Louisiana. It is the area in which the big, fat, beefsteak tomatoes grow wild. They taste wild.

1 large round eggplant (aubergine)	1 tbl double cream
2 eggs, beaten	oil for deep frying
1 cup (5 oz/125 g) seasoned dry breadcrumbs	1 cup (5 oz/125 g) catfish (or other white
6 tbl (3 oz/75 g) butter	freshwater fish)
1 cup (8 fl oz/250 ml) Creole sauce (see p. 42)	8 oysters
½ cup (4 fl oz/125 ml) dry white wine	12 shrimp
1 tbl soy sauce	2 cups (10 oz/250 g) crawfish

SERVES 4

Slice the skin from the eggplant and cut it into four 3/4-inch (2 cm) thick slices. Hollow out each slice into an egg-cup shape, the deeper the better. Take your time doing this. Use a teaspoon and ensure you do not break through the flesh. When all four are ready, dip into the beaten eggs and then into seasoned breadcrumbs. Repeat until covered, then chill.

Melt the butter, add the other sauce ingredients, cream last. Keep the temperature below a simmer. Add catfish, as soon as they are cooked, add all other seafood, turn off heat and cover with lid. Don't touch.

Heat oil deep enough to fry up to 350°F/180°C. Drop eggplant cups into oil, fry for 5 minutes. Drain. Place cups on plates. Stir sauce well. Fill each cup with an equal share of seafood, then smother in sauce.

Oyster Pan Roast

This is quick, easy and beautiful. The oysters have to be fresh, the opposite is frozen.

If you are having an intimate dinner, this oyster dish, a nice bottle of French Chardonnay – lighter than the New World varieties – and a crusty baguette are all you will need for a successful time.

The first time I ate a pan roast was at The Oyster Bar in Grand Central Station, Manhattan, a glorious venue. I was expecting a sort of bouillabaisse. When the roast arrived I was too scared to say they had messed up my order. Then, on eyeing the other customers, I realized this creamy, velvety soup was my roast. Enjoy.

16 shucked oysters (retain and strain the liquor)   *1 tsp paprika*
Good splash of wine (about 2 fl oz/60 ml)   *1 tsp Worcestershire Sauce*
3 tbl (1½ oz/45 g) melted butter   *2 tsp soy sauce*
2 tbl chili sauce   *2 cups (16 fl oz/500 ml) double cream*

A RECIPE FOR TWO

Make a broth with the oyster liquid and the rest of the ingredients. Add the oysters, cook just until edges curl (do not let the liquid boil) and serve.

Stuffed Flounder Pontchartrain with Shrimp Butter

Here we go, another semantic nightmare. When is a flounder not a flounder? When is it a sole? Got me. My fishing encyclopedia says 'any one of three families of flatfish, representing more than 200 species in the Atlantic and Pacific oceans, from the tiny dab to the gigantic halibut.' Great.

Well, firstly forget plaice. They are too dull. If you are in the States, find black-back flounder. In Britain, I reckon any sole is fine. Turbot and halibut taste the best, but are generally too big for this dish. You should do your own dressing of the fish or make sure the fishmonger does it very carefully.

2 saltwater white fish (each weighing 12oz/
    750 g)
½ small white onion, grated
½ small red onion, grated
1 scallion (spring onion), finely chopped
2 tbl (1 oz/25 g) butter
2 tbl lemon juice
6 tbl (3 oz/75 g) mushrooms, diced small

1 tbl crabmeat
1 egg yolk
1 tbl breadcrumbs
2 tbl parsley, finely chopped
2 tbl Parmesan, grated
1 tsp garlic salt
1 tsp ground white pepper
½ tsp cayenne

A RECIPE FOR TWO

Remove head and guts of each fish. Slice down backbone, but no further. Run your knife along top of the skeleton to edges. Do not cut through. It is then easy to cut the edge bones; you can even use scissors, the bones are thin. Now run the knife under the skeleton, it will be easy to work loose now.

Keep the knife as close to bone as possible. If you do remove some of the flesh by accident, scrape it off and add it to the stuffing mix. Place fish in fridge and prepare the stuffing mix. If you took your time you should have a perfect 'pocket' of a fish.

Sauté the onions and scallion in butter for 3-4 minutes. Add salt and pepper, half the lemon juice, and the mushrooms. Cook for a further few minutes, keep stirring. Remove from the heat and fold in crabmeat, then the egg yolk and breadcrumbs. Season with half the garlic salt, cayenne and white pepper.

Fill each fish cavity with the stuffing. Sprinkle with the rest of the lemon juice, the parsley, and parmesan in that order. Then sprinkle with the rest of the seasoning. Bake on an oiled baking tray for 20 minutes or so at 350°/180°C/gas mark 4.

Other ingredients I have added to the stuffing mix are oyster sauce, mustard seeds, cilantro, and chopped bacon.

I prefer this dish served with shrimp butter and freshly-baked rolls. I do however, appreciate that some people like sauces with fish. If this is the case I would offer lemon butter sauce. I love lemon butter sauce. It is by far the most accessible and most acceptable, providing you use unsalted butter. Many fish at Kenny's have been served with it and it is great with soft-shell crabs. Occasionally, I would funk it up with diced red jalapeños and call it Spiked Lemon Butter.

Lemon Butter Sauce

3/4 cup (6 oz/150 g) unsalted butter
1 small white onion, grated
1 tbl lemon juice
A good splash or two (about 4 fl oz/125 ml) dry
   white wine

1/2 cup (4 fl oz/125 ml) double cream
1 tbl parsley, finely chopped
1 tsp garlic salt
1 tsp ground white pepper

Melt butter and add onion, sauté for 3 minutes. Add wine and parsley. After a few minutes, add seasoning. Taste. Slowly mix in cream and bring back to a simmer. The sauce will only take 2-3 minutes to reach desired thickness.

Finely grated lemon zest can strengthen the flavor and also contribute to presentation. If the butter starts to 'leak' and look oily, take the pan off the heat and give the sauce a good beating with your wooden spoon. Always keep a little wine handy in case it starts to stick.

Shrimp Butter

Shrimp butter is delicious. This flavored butter is also easy to make with crawfish, crab, or lobster. You may wish to make a little extra to use as a spread on toast. I sometimes add red fish roe to the butter for extra color.

Bring some butter to room temperature. If you have the luxury of shrimp or crawfish shells available, boil them up for a stock. If not use fish stock or clam juice. In a blender or food processor, combine a few shelled and de-veined cooked shrimp with sautéed onion, parsley, and garlic. After a few pulses, start to dribble enough stock to make a fairly loose mixture. Blend for another 2 minutes max. Add garlic salt and coarsely ground black pepper. Beat the shrimp mixture into the softened butter. Chill until firm.

Another butter I enjoy making is Bajan Bullies' Butter. It is simply softened butter mixed with jalapeños, cumin, tomato purée, fresh cilantro, and sea salt. Always chill it in the containers in which it is to be served.

Trout Marguéry

Trout Marguery is a very popular dish in New Orleans. I was not going to include my version as I seldom come across wild trout, and farmed are not even worth deep-frying. You may be luckier than me so here it is. You could always substitute another fish, such as sole, sea-trout or sea-bream.

4 trout fillets
3 cups (1 lb/450 g) fresh mushrooms, finely chopped
1 cup (8 fl oz/250 ml) double cream
1 cup (5 oz/125 g) cooked, shelled, de-veined shrimp or white crabmeat

½ tsp onion salt
½ tsp black pepper, freshly ground
2 egg yolks, beaten
2 tbl (1 oz/25 g) melted butter

SERVES 4

Roll the trout fillets around two fingers and hold the turbans in place with toothpicks. Arrange them in a greased roasting pan, and bake at 350°F/180°C/gas mark 4 for 15 minutes. Meanwhile, make a cream sauce with mushrooms and shrimp and/or crab. Add the seasoning. Pull the trout from oven. Add egg yolks and melted butter to sauce, off the heat, stir well, return to the heat and cook until almost boiling but do not let it boil or it will curdle. Then pour it over the trout.

Another trout dish I like, which was on our first menu, is Pecan-Roasted Trout. Remove head, remove bones, and you will be left with a 'fan.' Season the fish, cover in crushed pecans, dot with butter, and broil (grill). I served this with a Creole sauce to which I added cream and white wine. My mother loved it.

A popular preparation for fish, usually trout, in the older restaurants of New Orleans such as Galatoire's, is 'méunière,' pronounced 'moon-yehr.' The trout fillets are lightly dusted with flour, sautéed in butter, and served with a lemon beurre noir. Dull.

Pompano en Papillote

Pompano to most of us ichthyophiles (fishheads) is the yardstick for all other saltwater fish. In Louisiana, there is not even a debate. Do not confuse them with Permit or Pomfret. They don't compare, except in appearance. They are all members of the Jack family.

The Permit is a mercurial fish in its own right, highly sought-after by sports fishermen. Especially off the Florida Keys (Cays). They are as strong as hell's attraction and are vicious fighters. Mark Twain called Pompano as 'delicious as the lesser forms of sin.' Sounds good, eh? The most famous way to prepare the fish is 'en papillotte,' often a mess of a dish in New Orleans, one which is used to trick tourists into saying goodbye to many greenbacks. But it need not be.

This dish was created by the owner of Antoine's restaurant, Jules Alciatore. He is credited with many inspirational dishes. I am sure he must have stolen his ideas from somewhere, either that or he partook of the mind-bending absinthe – the Green Muse – which was popular in the Crescent City until it was banned in 1912.

Apparently the dish was created to celebrate the feat of a Brazilian balloonist, Alberto Santos-Dumant. You will understand why on reading the recipe. It became such a New Orleans classic that the movie director Cecil B. de Mille wrote the dish into the movie *The Pirate's Lady*, despite the fact that the story is supposed to take place even before Antoine's opened in 1840. But hey, who cares? It's a great dish and works fine with sole or flounder fillets, since you may not be able to get Pompano outside the U.S. Pompano en Papillotte also allows you a fun presentation at the table, if you execute it right that is. Elegant but easy.

1 pompano fillet (use sole or flounder if not available), I prefer skin on
½ cup (5 oz/125 g) chopped mushrooms
1 scallion (spring onion)
6 tbl (3 oz/75 g) butter
1 tsp onion salt
1 tsp ground white pepper

1 tsp paprika
3 medium shrimp, diced
5 tbl (2½ oz/60 g) picked white crabmeat
1 tbl parsley, finely chopped
About 1 cup (5 oz/125 g) seaweed (dulse) or samphire (optional)

SERVES 2

Sauté mushroom and scallion in 2 oz/50 g butter for five minutes. Remove from heat and add seasoning and shrimp, and mix well. Then add crabmeat. Dot top of fillet with the rest of the butter and cover with crabmeat mixture.

Assemble the 'papillotte' (see below), place in fish and seal. Bake at 350°F/180°C/gas mark 4 for 30-40 minutes. If you can find seaweed (dulse) or samphire, place it in 'papillotte' too, it will add flavor and aroma, plus a vibrant color.

For the 'papillotte'; draw a valentine heart on a piece of greaseproof paper. Cut it out. Fold the heart in half, to give you an ear shape. Butter the inside, place the fillet on one side. Crimp tightly together the edges of the paper. Now it is ready to bake. Once the cooking has finished, serve the dish to each guest whilst still in the bag. This is fun and will also ensure the fish is fully cooked.

Crawdads

'You get a line and I'll get a pole
You get a line and I'll get a pole, babe
You get a line and I'll get a pole
And we'll go down to the crawdad hole
Honey, babe mine...'

The story of the Acadians I documented earlier. When they decided to leave the Northeast, they had to tell their friends the lobsters, with whom they had coexisted ever since their arrival, of their plans. The King of the lobsters discussed this horror with his people and they also decided to leave with their friends. Consequently, the Acadians tied pieces of string to the crustaceans and set off for Louisiana, heading for a new life.

It was a long trip. By the time they arrived the lobsters had lost so much weight they were pitiful little things, only a fraction of their original size. But like the Acadians, they were in their new homes and happy to stay. They have remained in the muddy bayous and marshlands ever since, never returning to their original size.

Crawfish or crawdads, known erroneously outside the South as crayfish, are freshwater crustaceans, which look like miniature versions of the rock lobster and taste like sweet shrimp.

Crawfish are incredibly popular in South Louisiana. Just about everyone eats them, in a multitude of different dishes. The most popular is crawfish boil, in which whole, live crawfish are thrown into a huge pot of boiling water flavored with herbs and spices. They are eaten with the fingers. I always had trouble selling Crawfish Boil because as a restaurant dish it is rather too messy, but it is the highlight of many a Louisiana party. Spread the newspaper thick, provide buckets of ice-cold beer, and enjoy.

Crawfish are found on every continent, except Africa. The U.S. has a hundred species, Louisiana alone has 29 species. But in crawfish country it is only the Red Swamp variety which is sought after. (Although the White is eaten too).

Crawfish country is Cajun country, the 22 parishes (Louisiana's equivalent of counties) from Simmesport to Lafayette and down to the Gulf, the home of the Atchafalaya Basin and the lower tributaries of the Mississippi. Good swampy surroundings for a multitude of animals, from 'gators to turtles and egrets to crawdads.

The best way to catch your own crawfish is to place an open tin of catfood in the center of a bicycle wheel. Place the wheel in your favorite fishing hole. Drag it out after 3 or 4 beers and 'hello mudbugs!' Remember to purge them of mud for a day or two, before you eat them. They 'get off' on burrowing.

Crawfish are especially good when cooked in the crawfish 'fat', the liver which is so enriching to any dish. Thus, if you can buy the feisty crawdads, try and either buy them alive, healthy and whole, or buy the tail meat with the fat included. If you are lucky, you may be able to find them at specialist fishmongers, imported from Louisiana or Turkey.

Crawfish Boil

10 lb/5 kg crawfish (including crabs and shrimp
   as you feel like it)
8 pints/4.8 litres water
4 corn on the cob, cut in quarters
3 medium sweet potatoes, thickly sliced
3 medium white onions, sliced thick with skin on

2 pints/1.2 litres beer
6 lemons, halved
½ cup (2½ oz/60 g) cayenne
½ cup (2½ oz/60 g) garlic salt
½ cup (2½ oz/60 g) white pepper
2 tbl mustard seeds

I always allow two pounds of crawdaddies per guest. Therefore the recipe is for really no more than 6 folk.

Boil water with all vegetables and seasonings for 20 minutes. Don't check seasoning - no point. Drop in crawdads, carefully. They may wriggle a bit, but don't worry they soon forget. Keep cooking at boiling until all crawfish are vivid red. Remove all ingredients and let steam for a while. Your guests will be going crazy with anticipation. Keep the pot simmering until the cooking liquid is well reduced.

To serve, pour cooking liquid over the crawfish, then transfer to newspaper or a large platter. Invite guests to help themselves and allow yourself a pull on a cold beer, them tell them how to eat the crustaceans. Crack the head off, suck it, inside is the flavorful fat. Discard the head. Hold the tail end in one hand and crack the shell along each side, in half-twisting motion. This should allow you to pull out the meat and hopefully the black vein. Enjoy.

Crawfish Etouffée

Etouffée (ay-too-FAY) is essentially an old-fashioned way of cooking. The word literally means to 'smother.'

You place the main ingredient (meat or fish) in a heavy-based pan with a tight-fitting lid over a low flame and cover the meat or fish with a layer of finely chopped vegetables. With the lid tightly in place, allow the ingredients to sweat together for hours.

Today most folk cheat, including me. To approximate the thick, hearty sauce the etouffée cooking process creates, make a roux-based sauce. Then sauté the chosen product to order in garlic and onions and finally smother it with the sauce. An etouffée dish is always served over white rice.

Freddie Fruge from Eunice, Louisiana, is the final word on etouffée. He adds cream of celery soup to his recipe. I am not bold enough to do that, but etouffée was always one of the top five sellers. We offered a variety of styles, but chicken, steak, shrimp, and naturally, crawfish, were the most popular.

2 cups (1 lb/450 g) crawfish tails, with fat hopefully
2 pints/1.2 litres chicken stock
1 pint/600 ml seafood stock
2 tbl Cajun seasoning (p. 19)
½ cup (4 fl oz/125 ml) roux (p. 21)
1 tbl tomato purée
2 tbl (1 oz/25 g) butter
2 cloves garlic, finely chopped
1 small white onion, grated

3 cups (1 lb/450 g) hot cooked white rice, drained
4 tbl parsley, finely chopped

FOR THE TRINITY

1 cup (5 oz/125 g) green bell pepper, coarsely chopped
1 cup (5 oz/125 g) celery, coarsely chopped
1 cup (5 oz/125 g) white onion, coarsely chopped

SERVES 4-6

Boil up the stocks together. Add trinity and one third of Cajun seasoning. Cook for 15-20 minutes and add roux. After 30 minutes, add second third of seasoning. Lower to a simmer, add tomato purée, and rest of seasoning. After 20 minutes take from the heat but keep stirring.

Sauté the crawfish, with fat hopefully, in garlic and grated onion. Pack the rice into individual molds. Unmold the rice on each plate, portion the crawfish around the molds and spoon the étouffée sauce over them. Garnish with finely chopped parsley.

To make a traditional etouffée - sauté the trinity in lots of butter for an hour with seasonings, garlic, and a dash of Worcestershire Sauce. Cover the pot with a tight-fitting lid. Add the crawfish and cook, covered, for another hour. Stir in chopped scallions and chopped parsley. Serve.

In Louisiana they have a children's folk hero called Clovis. She's a crawfish.

Angel Hair Pasta with Crawfish and Tasso

Angel hair pasta or vermicelli (allow 1-2 oz/
  25-50 g per person)
6 tbl (3 oz/75 g) butter
1 medium red onion, grated
3 scallions (spring onions), chopped
1 small red bell pepper, cut real small
About 1 cup (8 fl oz/250 ml) white wine
1 tbl soy sauce

2 cups (10 oz/250 g) crawfish tails
2½ cups (1 pint/600 ml) chicken stock
1 tsp garlic salt
1 tsp garlic, finely chopped
1 cup (5 oz/125 g) tasso, finely chopped
2 egg yolks
1 tbl parsley, finely chopped

SERVES 2-4 FOLK

This dish has to be executed fast. Melt the butter and sauté onions and bell pepper, keep dashing in wine, we want a creamy sauce. Add soy sauce and tails. Remove from heat, while still stirring until cool.

Cook pasta in stock with garlic, garlic salt, tasso, and parsley. As soon as the pasta is al dente, strain the egg yolks and beat them in. Arrange the pasta on a plate and keep it warm. Pour crawfish sauce over pasta and liberally sprinkle with parsley.

A neat veggie dish along the same lines is noodles tossed with melted butter, grated fresh ginger, and tomato salsa. Garnish with chopped, unsalted, dry-roasted peanuts.

Crawfish Pie

I find it easiest to make these pies in individual pie dishes or ramekins, although it is possible to make a large pie. I also like baking crawfish pies as turnovers, much in the same way as a Natchitoches Meat Pie (see p. 154), my favorite being 'Oysters Rockefeller Turnover.' Consequently, I will leave the pastry side of things to you, you may just want to make the sauce and eat it with buttermilk bisquits (a sort of Southern-style savory scone, see p. 153).

If you can't find clamato juice, substitute seafood stock.

1 tbl medium-colored roux (see p. 21)

1 tbl parsley, finely chopped

½ tsp oregano

½ tsp basil

½ tsp cayenne

½ tsp garlic salt

½ tsp garlic powder

1 tbl lemon juice

2 cups (16 fl oz/500 ml) clamato juice

1 tbl tomato purée

5 scallions (spring onions), chopped

6 cups (2 lb/900 g) crawfish tails

3 cups (1 lb/450 g) ready-made shortcrust dough
  for the pies

FOR THE TRINITY

1 cup (5 oz/125 g) green bell pepper, coarsely
  chopped

1 cup (5 oz/125 g) celery, coarsely chopped

1 cup (5 oz/125 g) white onion, coarsely chopped

SERVES 4 GUESTS

Heat up the roux. Sauté trinity, parsley, and seasonings in the roux for five minutes. Add lemon juice and slowly pour in clamato juice. Add the tomato purée, bring to simmer, add scallions and crawfish, and remove from heat. Leave to cool and then construct pies as you wish.

Crawfish Trixie

I love this nearly as much as my Blue Cheese Pecan Balls. It is named after a strange friend of mine from Fayetteville, Arkansas.

3 cups (1 lb/450 g) crawfish tails

1 small red onion, grated

1 small red jalapeño chile, finely diced

2 tbl (1 oz/25 g) butter

1 tsp garlic salt

1 tsp cayenne

¾ cup (6 fl oz/175 ml) double cream

½ cup (4 fl oz/125 ml) fish stock

Toast triangles for serving

A STARTER FOR 4-6

Sauté onion and chile in butter. Add seasoning and cream, keep cooking, and add the stock. Once thick, add crawfish, quickly heat up, and serve over toast.

A similar dish is Shrimp Newburg Teche. Just add sherry and paprika, and maybe scallions.

Or make my Spanish Crawfish Sauté, which is crawfish tails dredged in flour then sautéed in butter with rum, nutmeg, cinnamon, and chives. Serve over grilled cornbread.

BBQ Shrimp New Orleans Style

Do not prepare this dish if any of your guests has just had a manicure, or even if they are disposed to have one. I once had dinner at the Gulf Coast, a restaurant in New York City. One of the guys brought along his new girl. Big hair, too much perfume, and perfectly new nails. You know the type. She ordered BBQ Shrimp, New Orleans Style – big mistake lady! New Orleans style means in their shells, head on, swimming in a buttery, peppery mess of sauce and served only with a French stick for sopping, up the liquid.

6 cups (2 lb/900 g) shrimp, head and shell on,
   bigger the better
1 medium red onion, grated
4 cloves garlic, finely chopped
½ cup (4 fl oz/125 ml) olive oil
6 tbl (3 oz/75 g) butter
1 tbl black pepper, freshly ground
1 tsp onion salt

1 cup (8 fl oz/250 ml) red wine
1 tbl Worcestershire Sauce
1 tbl soy sauce
1 tbl lemon juice
Parsley, finely chopped
Crusty baguette
Green salad

SERVES 4 FOLK

Sauté onion and garlic in oil for 5 minutes, add butter, pepper, and onion salt. Cook on high heat then add wine, Worcestershire Sauce, soy sauce, and lemon juice. Boil up again then add shrimp. As soon as they are pink, serve.

To serve, distribute between bowls and pour the sauce over it. The sauce should be sloppy and very peppery. Garnish with chopped parsley and serve with bread and salad. Provide paper napkins and tell your guests not to be timid.

The Beautiful Swimmer

Louisiana Crabcakes were the favorite of many a Kenny's customer. Virtually every review we had mentioned them. They never made me much money, but boy! They were excellent. We tried to use only Callinectus sapidus, the beautiful swimmer, or more simply the Blue Crab.

Initially we imported picked blue crabmeat from Myers in Louisiana, along with gumbo crabs, crawfish tails, and alligator meat. Unfortunately the source dried up, Brunnings, the importer, went bust and no-one else was crazy enough to import them. Brunnings was a great importer and fishmonger. Whatever I wanted arrived, be it speckled trout, opah, rock shrimp, tautog, spearfish, surf clams, or hog snapper. But, as the crab source dried up, we began to use English brown crabs, which are similar to stone crabs.

It is not easy to explain cooking and dressing live crabs. Particularly as all crabs, wherever they are from, produce different grades of meat depending upon weather and conditions. Not the fisherman's fault, or ours, or the crabs'. Thus I will suggest you don't bother and just use good quality picked crabmeat.

One point though, if you dress your own crabs, do not miss the covering inside of the main shell, it is ambrosia. Cooking and dressing crabs was a real bore each morning. I always did the bulk of it myself. Firstly, because cooking time was vital, and breaking up the crab was important to the customer's health. And I wanted to run my finger around the back of that shell!

Truly outrageous. (It was also an expensive item to waste.)

In Maryland they say scream for capers and forget onions and shallots. Other way around for me. At the Commander's Palace Restaurant in New Orleans, they add Romaine cheese, but that's not for me either. You may want to experiment with those sorts of ideas.

So here is my favorite recipe. It's easy, but I cannot overemphasize the need to ensure your crabmeat is fresh, a good-to-excellent grade. Consequently never, ever, overcook your patties. This applies to most food, but to seafood most of all.

If you can dress your own crabs, or you source some 'blinding' crabmeat please do not stretch it. Keep the portions small and fill the plate with garnish or Creole sauce. Your guests will look for more.

If you want a top class venue at which to savor real crabs you need to head for the States – probably true for most seafood. Britain has really lost it. The best concentration of crab houses is found I guess, in Baltimore. A back-to-basics sort of a place, where you become part of the scenery, just by eating steamed crabs in the ritual manner, pounding the freshly-steamed critters with wooden mallets, etc...

Some would say – and who am I to argue? – that the most famous and traditional house is Gunnings, in Brooklyn, Baltimore the most eclectic part of the city. Passing Lonnie's Bolero Lounge and the Headquarters of Taxidermy, you find Gunnings opposite Bob's Furniture and the Sno-Ball Shack. Like all the best restaurants, as soon as you are through the door, there is an arresting smell, this time of crab and spices, and you are faced with a loud, busy bar. This leads to the dining room, where the decor is kitsch – red checkered tablecloths, etc. You order. Brown wrapping paper is spread in front of you, with pitchers of beer and water, followed by a huge tray of steamed crabs. Hammer away. The Devil would enjoy this place, not to mention Maenad.

According to the Maryland Seafood Association, Baltimore has around 300 crab houses. It's easy to imagine that the debate as to the best venue is a complex and tetchy one. Some say Bo Brooks in the northern part of the city is the best. It is certainly busy, though the oldest is Obryckis. But just like oyster-eating, it is important to choose a busy joint.

Louisiana Crabcakes with Creamed Creole Sauce

2-3 lb/900 g-1 kg crabmeat
½ tsp paprika
1 tsp cayenne
½ tsp garlic salt
½ tsp coarse-ground black pepper
1 cup (5 oz/125 g) homemade crumbs, made from stale bread, crushed saltines, or Ritz crackers

1 cup (8 fl oz/250 ml) mayonnaise
½ cup (4 fl oz/125 ml) coarse-grained mustard
5 egg yolks (keep the whites for Caesar salad dressing or Mile High Ice Cream Pie (see pp. 185 and 230)
Large dash Worcestershire Sauce
Large dash lemon juice

SERVES 4-6

If you can find Old Bay Seasoning in the UK, use it. The food halls of the big department stores may stock it occasionally, or get a friend to send some over from the U.S.

It is possible to either broil or sauté these patties. Your choice. Mix your seasonings with the breadcrumbs. Mix mayonnaise and mustard, then add to breadcrumbs, mixing with a wooden spoon. Then add egg yolks, Worcestershire Sauce, and lemon juice. Mix lightly but thoroughly. Add crabmeat and fold in. Form patties to the desired size. I could tell you how many to make, but where's the fun in that, eh?

Squeeze the patties into shape and chill, this facilitates easier cooking. Cook about 30 minutes after chilling; too long in the refrigerator will destroy some of the flavor.

I prefer to sauté the crabcakes in butter over a high heat but, of course, the cooking is up to you. If you don't fancy a sauce, maybe a tomato salad, drizzled with olive oil, will suffice. The flavors will not appreciate too much bombardment, consequently do not overcook.

I guess you can work out Creamed Creole Sauce. Mix your Creole Sauce (see p. 42) with ½ cup (4 fl oz/125 ml) double cream, ½ cup (4 fl oz/125 ml) white wine, 2 tbl (1 oz/25 g) butter and a couple of chopped scallions.

Louisiana Crab-Stuffed Avocado with Crab Dressing

Down in Louisiana they love stuffing foods, and they are especially fond of using seafood as stuffing. There are shrimp-stuffed mushrooms, pompano en papillotte, gumbo poopah, stuffed flounder, crawfish bisque, broiled stuffed shrimp, stuffed crabs Lafitte, and so on. I have cooked them all and would love to have included my own versions for you. Maybe next time.

Crab-stuffed avocado was on our first menu, I felt obliged to make my own stuffed dish. What we are doing here is making a crab stuffing, which we mix with avocado flesh and top with parmesan. The dish is then baked. It can be served cold or hot, but I suggest you serve it straight from the oven. In case your 'alligator pears' do not want to sit still, cut off the 'pointiest' side of the skin. They should oblige, with a little squish. One point about avocados – it is not worth worrying about their high fat content as it's mostly the monounsaturated variety.

6 ripe avocados

About 4 tbl olive oil

1 medium white onion, grated

2 scallions (spring onions), finely chopped

1 cup (5 oz/125 g) mushrooms, finely chopped

½ cup (2½ oz/60 g) crabmeat

½ cup (2½ oz/60 g) shrimp, diced

1 tsp Worcestershire Sauce

1 tsp cayenne

1 tsp onion salt

1 tsp paprika

1 tsp oyster sauce

Parmesan cheese

4 tbl parsley, finely chopped

About 2 tbl (1 oz/25 g) butter

SERVES 6

Pit and halve the avocados carefully, keeping the shells intact. Remove half the flesh and mash it, then return it to the shells.

Heat the oil and sauté onion and mushroom. Add seasoning, shrimp and crab, cook for a couple of minutes. Remove from heat. Add Worcestershire Sauce and oyster sauce, mix and cool. Mix in the spare half of avocado flesh. Then fill each avocado shell with the stuffing. Cover with Parmesan, sprinkle with parsley, and dot with butter.

Bake at 350°F/180°C/gas mark 4 for 10-15 minutes, until Parmesan becomes 'dry.'

Stuffed Mirliton

You can stuff a mirliton in the same way you stuff an avocado. Among the ancient Mayans of central America, this vegetable was called 'chayote.' In some places it still is. Most people call it chow-chow, custard marrow, christophine, xuxu, or vegetable pear. But the Creoles know it and love it as the mirliton. It belongs to the same family as cucumbers and squash. On its own it has a very bland flavor, but that makes it perfect for blending with similarly light ingredients, such as crab, shrimp or vegetables.

Try to use the female mirliton, it has a smoother skin. Simmer the whole vegetable in salted water for 17 minutes until it can be pierced easily with a fork. Leave it to cool and scoop out the flesh without breaking the skin.

Cook up wild rice with garlic, mix with diced shrimp, and grated red onions. Stuff the mirliton and cover with breadcrumbs, dot with butter and bake at 350°F/180°C/gas mark 4 for 30-40 minutes.

Cornmeal-Fried Catfish with Hush Puppies

At Kenny's, being a Southern joint, fried catfish was big news. Maybe because the birthright of the catfish is unimpeachable. Naturally I had to play with the simple Cornmeal-Fried version with Hush Puppies, although I preferred Mustard-Fried Catfish. This is not a difficult recipe, but nonetheless due to its position as the behemoth of Southern cooking I am sharing with you the recipe cited by the Catfish Institute of Mississippi as being 'the' Classic Fried Catfish. The Institute represents catfish growers from Mississippi, Louisiana, Alabama, and Arkansas, all working hard to ensure their fish are of consistently high quality. I'm a big fan.

3/4 cup (6 oz/175 g) cornmeal
2 tbl plain flour
2 tsp salt
1 tsp cayenne

1/4 tsp garlic powder
4 farmed catfish fillets
Vegetable oil

SERVES 4

Sift dry ingredients together. Coat each fish, shake off excess. Heat oil to 350°F/180°C and shallow-fry each fish for 5-6 minutes.

Hush Puppies

Wherever there is fried fish in the Deep South you will find hush puppies. Apparently, whilst cooking up a 'fry,' the cook would drop batches of cornmeal batter into the hot oil and with the admonition, 'Now hush up, puppies,' throw the resulting fritters to the yapping dogs who were loitering in the kitchen in the hope of getting fed.

1 cup (10 oz/250 g) cornmeal
2 tsp baking powder
½ cup (2½ oz/60 g) self-raising flour
1 tbl sugar
1 egg

1 onion, finely chopped
½ green bell pepper
1 red jalapeño, finely chopped
1 cup (8 fl oz/250 ml) milk
Vegetable oil for frying

Combine all the ingredients. Drop spoonfuls into hot oil and fry until golden.

Mustard-Fried Catfish with Sauce Nantua

Catfish is the fifth most popular fish consumed in the States, after tuna, pollock, cod, and salmon. This represents 439 million pounds of farmed raised catfish. No longer seafood's poor country cousin, farmed catfish has become one of America's most popular and versatile foods.

6 catfish fillets
1 cup (5 oz/125 g) dry mustard
1 cup (5 oz/125 g) plain flour
2 tsp garlic salt
2 tsp coarsely ground black pepper

2 eggs
1¼ cups (10 fl oz/300 ml) milk
1 tbl parsley, finely chopped
5 tbl (2 oz/60 g) chopped pecans (optional)
1 small red jalapeño, diced small (optional)

Combine the dry mustard, flour, garlic salt, and pepper. Beat the eggs add and mix with the milk. Add dry to wet and beat into a batter. You can either fry the fish as is, or dredge it in cornmeal, to which you have added chopped pecans and one small red jalapeño, diced real small.

Sauce Nantua

Crawfish (crawdads) are freshwater crustaceans which look like miniature rock lobsters. They are found all over the world in unpolluted lakes and rivers and have an extremely delicate flavor. They may be hard to find in the United Kingdom, since they are mostly exported. Though there is really no substitute, you could use shrimp, lobster, or langoustine if you cannot find crawfish.

Breaux Bridge, Louisiana, calls itself the Crawfish Capital of the World, just as Gonzales, Louisiana is the Jambalaya Capital of the World. However, Nantua in France may take offense over Breaux Bridge's claim. Nantua is in Bugey, a district in Savoy where some of France's best cuisine is to be found. Brillat-Savarin was born there. A la Nantua is a name given to various dishes which are either garnished or cooked with crawfish. They enjoy their écrevisses down there too. I produce a rich velvety sauce with crawfish tails which I flavor with brandy in the traditional way. It may be a little too refined for fried catfish, but I enjoy contrasts.

3 cups (1 lb/450 g) crawfish tails (or, sadly,
  shrimp in their absence)
6 tbl (3 oz/75 g) butter
2 scallions (spring onions)
1 tsp sea salt
1 tsp coarse-ground black pepper

1 cup (8 fl oz/250 ml) fish stock
1 cup (8 fl oz/250 ml) white wine
1 tbl parsley, finely chopped
About 2 fl oz/60 ml brandy
½ cup (4 fl oz/125 ml) double cream

Sauté the crawfish in the butter and add the scallions. Cook for 3-4 minutes. Cool, then purée for 10 seconds in blender. Let the texture stay slightly coarse.

Add the seasonings to the stock and bring it to a boil. Cook five minutes then add the crawfish mix. After 3 minutes remove from heat. Mix in wine, parsley, and brandy, then cream. Stir for two minutes. Do not allow to boil or the cream will separate. If the sauce is too thin, reduce for a couple more minutes.

'How D'Ya Like Dem Ersters?'

My favorite oyster house in the world is The Acme in New Orleans, closely followed by the Oyster Bar at the Grand Central Station in New York City. The Oyster Bar and Restaurant at Grand Central Station was one of the terminal's original amenities when the station opened back in 1913 and it has never moved from its original spot, two storys below mid-town Manhattan, beneath what was once the historic Biltmore Hotel, now gone. The Oyster Bar has outlived this and many more salubrious edifices in the surroundings. Such is the might of the oyster, eh? All 10,000 a day which are opened here.

The menus are poster-sized and change daily. At the top is the list of available oysters - Chilmark, Wellfleet, James River, Kent Island, and Wescott Bay. Belons are occasionally available and the Blue Point is the 'house' oyster. The range of varieties available are based on environment, size, color and intensity of flavor. Various condiments are offered, but don't bother. 'Au naturel s'il vous plait.' What's the point, unless you don't care how good your oysters taste? Saying that, they do THE 'oyster roast,' mentioned earlier. - an oyster dish for the gods. And their fish list is certainly beyond compare.

Down in the French Quarter of the Big Easy, another of New Orleans' many names, we have the Acme Oyster House. It rivals anywhere, anywhere. But not for oysters however. Oysters in the South suck. Here you should eat the Red Beans or the Gumbo Poopah (gumbo served in a hollowed out loaf). You go to the Acme to have a good time. It is loud, funky, messy, and has the nastiest, dirtiest, scariest, most beautiful bar-tenders anywhere.

My favorite oyster dishes are Rockefeller, Kenny, Bienville, Rousseau, Ella and Jamie. The reputation of Oysters Rockefeller is huge yet few folk really know how to make it. It is basically assumed to be oysters baked with spinach and cheese. So wrong. The original dish was oysters cooked with watercress, scallions, anise, and seasoning. It was created by Jules

Alciatore in 1889. He owned the restaurant called Antoine's in New Orleans. His great grandson, Roy F.Guste, wrote in 'The Antoine's 1840 Cookbook' published in 1979, 'In 1899, there was a shortage of snails coming in from Europe to the US and Jules was looking for a replacement. He chose oysters . . . then he created a sauce with available greens, producing such a richness that he named it after one of the wealthiest men in the US, John D. Rockefeller.'

This is my version, having tried so many other people's recipes.

Oysters Rockefeller

12 oysters on the half shell
1 medium white onion, grated
3 scallions (spring onions), finely chopped
6 tbl (3 oz/75 g) butter
1 tsp white pepper
1 tsp garlic salt
About 1 cup (8 fl oz/250 ml) fish stock

1 tbl lemon juice
1 tsp Worcestershire Sauce
3 cups (1 lb/450 g) spinach, chopped
1 tbl Ricard, Pernod or Herbsaint
About 6 tbl (3 oz/75 g) grated Parmesan cheese
   (enough to cover all the shells)
Parsley, finely chopped

Loosen the oysters from the muscle but do not take them out of the shell. Sauté the onion and scallions in 4 tbl (2 oz/50 g) of the butter for 3 minutes. Add seasonings and a little fish stock, lemon juice, and Worcestershire Sauce, and cook for five more minutes. Remove from the heat and fold in spinach; keep folding until soft. Sprinkle Ricard over and gently re-heat. The spinach should be soft but not mushy. Keep adding small amounts of fish stock, but please take it easy.

Cover each oyster with a layer of the spinach mix, then cover with Parmesan, and finally sprinkle with the parsley. Place a couple of small flakes of cold butter over each oyster and broil under a hot grill until the sides of the shell begin to bubble. If the cheese is beginning to brown too fast, lower the heat.

It is easiest to serve the oysters on a bed of rock salt, for stability. If you have any blue or green food coloring knocking about, pour a small drop onto the salt. It absorbs the dye very well. You may want to get funky and serve the oysters on a bed of colored salt. Just don't go too garish (red doesn't work!)

Oysters Kenny

Back in London I invented a dish which ended up being called 'Oysters Kenny.' Inspirational huh? It was rather a weird discovery. I reckon very little in kitchens is actually defined by reason.

Oysters were always a big seller, but I became real bored with the simple 'on the half shell' presentation. Too many for breakfast, I guess. One afternoon, whilst having a break in the 'Nags Head,' I was reading an article on Chinese food and came across a new idea on how to serve oysters. An easy adaptation was to use my signature ingredients.

12 oysters on the half shell, opened just prior to serving.
1 cup (5 oz/125 g) tasso (smoked spicy ham, see p. 149)
1 medium red onion, very finely chopped
1 small red jalapeño, very finely chopped

2 tbl lemon juice
1 small green bell pepper, very finely diced
2 cloves garlic, finely chopped
1 tsp coarse-ground black pepper
1 tbl red wine vinegar
1 tsp garlic salt

Combine all ingredients, except the oysters, and chill for an hour.

Top each oyster with equal amounts of the 'Kenny' mix and leave for 5-10 minutes before serving.

Oysters Bienville

Oysters Bienville are oysters smothered with mushrooms and shrimp, then baked. Oysters Rousseau are similar using a herbed tomato sauce with onions and garlic, topped with bacon and baked as before. I enjoyed serving one of each, with an Oyster Kenny, as a portion. It tested my cooking ability and my guests' tastebuds. The platter looked groovy too.

This dish is dedicated to Jean Baptiste le Moyne, Sieur de Bienville, though not by me. He was the second colonial Governor of Louisiana. He died in 1768.

12 oysters
1 medium white onion, in small slices
3 scallions (spring onions), chopped
1 cup (8 oz/250 g) mushrooms, chopped
4 tbl (2 oz/50 g) butter
½ cup (4 fl oz/125 ml) white wine
1 tsp garlic salt

1 tsp coarse-ground black pepper
1 cup (8 fl oz/250 ml) clam juice, or rich fish
   stock
½ cup (4 fl oz/125 ml) double cream
8 medium shrimp, diced
½ cup (2½ oz/60 g) breadcrumbs
½ cup (2½ oz/60 g) grated Gruyère cheese

Sauté onion, scallions and mushrooms together for 5 minutes in butter. Add wine and simmer for 2 minutes, then add seasonings and clam juice, keep cooking and slowly mix in cream. As soon as it simmers, take off heat, add shrimp, mix and let cool. It should be nearly thick and the shrimp heading for pink. I'm sure you can work out what to do if it's not.

When the sauce has cooled, top each oyster with sauce, then breadcrumbs. Wait a couple of minutes to let the breadcrumbs settle then top with cheese. Broil for as long as it takes for the cheese to melt under the grill, this should be long enough for everything else to warm up and for the oysters to begin curling. We don't want them thoroughly cooked, the whole idea is to have a fresh tasting flavor, where the oysters are only just touched with the other flavors.

Oysters Rousseau

12 oysters on the half shell (again I suggest 3 per person)
1 medium red onion, grated
2 cloves garlic, finely chopped
2 tbl (1 oz/25 g) butter

3 rashers streaky bacon, diced and briefly fried
2 medium tomatoes, cored and chopped
Parmesan cheese
Parsley, finely chopped

Sauté onion and garlic for 3 minutes in butter then add bacon and remove from heat. Add seasonings and tomatoes, mix well, then return to heat. Cook until tomatoes are soft. Top each oyster with the mixture and then sprinkle with cheese, and finish with the chopped parsley. Broil (grill) for 4-6 minutes.

Oysters Ella

Following the birth of my brother's daughter, I created a special dish for her, in true restaurateur fashion. It is oysters on the half shell topped with crabmeat which has been sautéed in garlic and sherry and then smothered in a spicy hollandaise sauce. Depending on size of the 'ersters, three per person should be fine. I prefer to use red onions for dishes that are only lightly cooked. They have a sweeter flavor.

12 oysters on the half shell.
1 large red onion
3 cloves garlic, finely chopped
2 small red jalapeños, finely diced

1 tbl sherry
1 tsp nutmeg
3 cups (1 lb/450 g) white crabmeat
Spicy Hollandaise Sauce (see p. 195)

I guess you can work out how to make the Hollandaise spicy, although I do suggest you add paprika as well for color.

Sauté onion, garlic, and jalapeños in butter for 4 minutes. Add sherry and nutmeg, mix in, then remove from heat and fold in crabmeat. Top each oyster with the mix and then with the Hollandaise.

Sprinkle with paprika. Quickly broil, the Hollandaise ought not to cook again. It will not take long for the sauce to begin bubbling, which is the time to serve and enjoy.

Oysters Jamie

Following the birth of Ella's brother, I felt obliged to maintain sibling equality.

This is oysters fried in seasoned cornmeal, replaced in their shells, and topped with a) tomato salsa and b) homemade garlic-chive mayonnaise.

Depending on the size of your oysters, 3 may not be enough this time. Frozen Japanese oysters are actually the best for frying.

12-16 oysters, shucked if fresh, liquor reserved
1 cup (8 oz/250 g) cornmeal
1 egg, beaten
½ cup (4 fl oz/125 ml) milk

1 tsp garlic salt
1 tsp cayenne
About ½ cup (4 fl oz/125 ml) oil for frying

To make the cornmeal batter, combine the egg, milk and seasoning. Dip each oyster in the cornmeal batter, then fry in the oil. Replace the oysters in their shells. Top with the salsa and then the mayonnaise. Fit for a King.

Tomato Salsa

4 medium tomatoes, cored and finely chopped
1 small white onion, finely chopped
1 small green bell pepper, finely chopped

1 small red jalapeño, diced very small
1 tbl lemon juice

Garlic-Chive mayonnaise

1 cup (8 fl oz/250 ml) good quality store-bought
  mayonnaise
1 tbl lemon juice

1 tbl chives, snipped small
1 tsp white wine vinegar

Strain the reserved oyster liquid then add it to the mayonnaise. Combine the salsa ingredients and chill them, then do the same with the mayonnaise ingredients.

Whilst on the subject of sucking down oysters – when no-one is looking, try one of my favorite cocktails. the 'Oyster Shooter.' We used our own flavored vodka – Cajun vodka – jalapeños steeped in Absolut. Pour a healthy shot into a shot glass, drop in a freshly shucked erster, and top with Bloody Mary Mix (p. 207); add a dash of lemon juice. Retain the drink in your mouth for a wee while, mash the oyster with your teeth, and swill around. It is truly outrageous. But don't tell your guests what you have been up to – your smirk may get them thinking.

Cajun Angels in Devils' Blankets

Okay here we go, the real reason I wrote this damn book – the need to finally and officially tell the world how to cook 'Cajun Angels.' If you never came to Kenny's you will not understand, but please persevere, it will be worth the effort.

The first Halloween, the eve of All Saints Day, we celebrated at Kenny's was back in 1989. I had no real idea what to do for a menu. All I knew was that Americans celebrate the occasion in a serious way and we were expected to perform. Everybody dressed up, pumpkins were carved, the dry ice was purchased, and I put on the obligatory tape – Screaming Jay Hawkins singing 'I Put a Spell on You,' Dr John singing 'Mama Roux,' The Neville Brothers and their 'Yellow Moon,' LaVerne Baker belting out 'Soul on Fire,' etc. As for a menu – I was in a pickle. Ultimately, I just played with the usual ideas and created wacky names, such as Witches' Teeth, 'Gator Toes. Throughout, there was one idea which I liked. It was for shrimp wrapped in bacon.

Shrimp was already our best-selling item, in whatever guise. Wrapping it in bacon was an idea stolen from Angels on Horseback. I blackened the shrimp, because it was fun, and served them with remoulade sauce. We were already serving a salad called Shrimp Remoulade. They were a huge and immediate hit.

I have discussed blackening earlier, but I will reiterate, I don't feel it is for home cooking. Remoulade sauce was invented by Monsieur Escoffier, a French dude. It is a white mayonnaise-style sauce flavored with capers. Dull. The Creoles, as usual, funked it up. Here's my version. It may appear to be a rather long recipe, but it does last and will be enjoyable with all sorts of strongly-flavored foods. In fact, I suggest you make a good amount and use it in place of butter in your sandwiches.

Wrapping food in bacon is by no means special to 'Angels.' Chef Jasper

White, from Boston, does great things with medallions of tuna wrapped in bacon. Play with the idea is what I say.

6 rashers streaky bacon, trimmed of rind, cut into two strips
16 shrimp, peeled, with tail left on
1 cup (5 oz/125 g) blackening mix (see below)

About ¼ cup (2 fl oz/60 ml) olive oil
1 cup (8 fl oz/250 ml) Remoulade sauce (see below)
1 tbl parsley, finely chopped

The bacon rashers have to be thin and long. Wrap each shrimp in one length of bacon, from tail to head-end. Press firmly. Drop each shrimp in blackening mix and gently shake until covered. As soon as all the shrimp are covered, chill them.

Heat up a heavy-based frying pan, cover with a thin layer of olive oil, remove from the heat and count to 75. Then flick a drop of water or beer into the frying pan, if it spits back - good. If not re-heat a little. If it is smoking, cool the pan further.

Arrange portions of the Remoulade on the side of each of four small plates. Retrieve shrimp. Place the frying pan back on heat, add a little more oil, carefully add each shrimp. Cook each side for three minutes, don't play with them - never play with food. The seasoning on the outside of the bacon should be dry and the exposed end of the shrimp, white. If not cook a little more.

Place four shrimp on each plate, tails out, with the shrimp 'spoon' like, just the way we all enjoy sleeping. Right? Garnish with chopped fine parsley. Enjoy.

I hate having to search through cookbooks or magazines for concluding pieces of articles or for important additions to a dish, thus I will repeat the blackening mix here. I apologize for having to do this elsewhere in my book. I know you'll understand.

My Blackening Mix

3 tbl paprika
3 tbl thyme
2 tbl oregano
3 tbl cayenne

2 tbl coarse-ground black pepper
2 tbl garlic salt
1 tbl garlic powder

Mix well and cover. The main players are the thyme and paprika. Dried herbs in this mix are infinitely better than fresh, they burn best.

Remoulade Sauce

1 tbl white wine vinegar
1 cup (8 fl oz/250 ml) mayonnaise
2 cups (16 fl oz/500 ml) ketchup
½ cup (4 fl oz/125 ml) creamed horseradish
1 cup (8 fl oz/250 ml) coarse-grained mustard
1 tbl lemon juice
1 tbl Worcestershire Sauce
½ cup (2½ oz/60 g) celery, very finely diced

½ cup (2½ oz/60 g) scallion, diced small
½ cup (2½ oz/60 g) parsley, finely chopped
1 tbl cayenne
1 tbl garlic salt
1 tsp coarse-ground black pepper
1 tsp onion powder
1 tsp garlic purée

Combine all the ingredients well and chill. Please remember that the parsley needs to be chopped really fine. I think store-bought mayonnaise is okay but, in preference, homemade ketchup is best.

Broiled Shrimp with Shrimpers' Sauce and Frings

Throwing shrimp straight on to the 'barbie' is bit of a hit-and-miss affair. Unless, of course, you have an abundant supply of them. Consequently I suggest you take your time and cook the shrimp carefully.

Shrimpers' Sauce is my adaptation of a recipe found in *Mississippi Gulf Coast*, a guide written by the Federal Writers' Project in 1939. It is a tomato sauce made by southern shrimpers.

Shrimpers' Sauce

Marinate the shrimp of your choice in lemon juice, finely chopped parsley, and finely chopped garlic, for 2 hours. Grill to order. Smother the shrimp in the sauce and top with Frings.

8 jumbo shrimp	*1 tsp cayenne*
1 cup (5 oz/125 g) salt pork, diced	*1 tsp garlic salt*
1 small red onion, grated	*1 tsp dried thyme*
2 tomatoes, skinned, cored, and chopped	*1 tsp onion powder*
2 scallions, finely chopped	*1 cup (8 fl oz/250 ml) V-8 juice*

Sauté diced salt pork with grated red onion, cored tomatoes and scallions. Once the onion has wilted and the pork has started to change color, add cayenne, garlic salt, thyme and onion powder. Add the V-8 juice and reduce. Serve over shrimp.

To really make this funky, at home I poach small seafood dumplings in the sauce.

Frings

Frings are a mixture of French Fries and Onion Rings. Hence the name. I like to use them as a garnish giving height to dishes, but they are equally good as a side order.

These are fun but they can screw up your oil. It is best to drain most of the juice out of the onion, by which time of course, most of the flavor has gone too. If you have a mandolin slicer or can slice seriously fine, then you should be okay. Don't try and grate the onion.

2 large white potatoes
2 large white onions
About 1 cup (8 fl oz/ 250 ml) groundnut oil for
 frying

French Quarter Seasoning (equal measures of
 garlic salt, cayenne, and paprika)

Grate the potato and keep in water until needed, this stops it from turning gray. Slice the onion using a mandolin or carefully by hand. I know it is difficult, but aim to lose as little juice as possible.

Heat oil to 375°F/190°C. Place onions in mixing bowl and sprinkle a little flour over them. Dry the potatoes by squeezing in a tea-towel, and add to onions with a little olive oil. Toss together, using your fingers, and drop into oil in small batches. They are ready when brown; drain and sprinkle with seasoning.

'Gator Sausage

'I like elegance and style in fighting, but sometimes you just got
to get down and mix it with the 'gators.'

Many people scoffed when this surfaced on the menu. Regardless, it sold great. It never won the *Guardian* newspaper sausage competition however – not even a significant mention.

 95

I remember an occasion when carrying the cooked 'gator meat to the car in Hampstead, I tripped, spilling 25 lb/11 kg of 'gator meat down Flask Walk, a narrow passage off Heath Street. A passing collie dog had a very strange expression on his face as he scoffed up spicy alligator, the great denizen of the Louisiana bayou.

As an aside, 'gator meat contains around 22% protein, compared to 17% in choice rump steak, whilst the fat content ranges from 1%–5%, compared to 25% in rump steak.

5 lb/2 kg alligator meat, diced
2 lb/1 kg lean ground pork
3 cups (1 lb/450 g) pork liver, chopped
1 cup (4 oz/125 g) red jalapeños, finely chopped
1 cup (4 oz/125 g) red onion, finely chopped
1 cup (4 oz/125 g) scallions (spring onions),
    finely chopped

1 tbl chopped fresh sage
1 tbl garlic salt
1 tbl fresh garlic, finely chopped
1 tbl ground white pepper

Combine the meats and grind them together in a food processor. Mix jalapeños and onion, then mix the seasonings. Combine all the ingredients and leave them to chill.

Either form into patties or press into hog casings and form into sausage links weighing about 4 oz/125 g each.

These taste great if served with mashed potato, to which you add a tablespoon or so of horseradish sauce. Provide ample amounts of red wine gravy.

Fish Fingers with Cocktail Sauce and Tartar Sauce

In the States they have so many fast food joints it makes you feel ill, sad, and confused. In the majority of those that serve anything resembling fish 'cocktail sauce' is omnipresent. It is usually nothing more than cheap ketchup and creamed horseradish. But, there are real cocktail sauces and real recipes. Use them.

Fish fingers are actually a wonderful dish in their own right. Initially, I started to use them as a way of saving trimmings and soon realized they are just good and fun. Whoever said food shouldn't be fun? Probably some guy in a big white hat with a red star on each shoulder.

I first ate real fish fingers in Key West, at Turtle Kraals. Not a palais des gourmands, but a fine joint nonetheless. They are a fishy, finger-food version of fried chicken, and real groovy. Use any fish, but white is best. I prefer grouper – despite my mate Big Bob, 'no job', protesting they are only fit for pelicans. What's he know, eh?

You should note at this point that oily fish, e.g., mackerel, tuna, and herring, not white fish like cod, can make you brainier. Our brain seems to like the decosahexaenoic acid (DHA) in oily fish. Actually DHA is said to help many conditions – blood circulation and rheumatoid arthritis, and it increases visual awareness. Unfortunately its effect on the brain is limited to children under 9 months of age, so it is particularly useful when we are embryonic. The other advantages may, however, help you and me now.

Fish Fingers

12 oz/350 g strong textured white fish, 4 inch/
   10 cm strips (they don't need to be uniform)
1 cup (5 oz/125 g) cornmeal
4 tbl (2 oz/50 g) parsley, finely chopped
1 tsp sea salt

1 tsp coarse-ground black pepper
2 eggs, beaten
1 cup (8 fl oz/250 ml) milk
About 1 cup (8 fl oz/250 ml) oil for frying

Prepare a seasoned cornmeal with chopped parsley, sea salt and coarse ground black pepper. Make a simple egg and milk batter. Dredge fish in batter then in cornmeal and fry straight away. They don't take long to fry, just until the batter is crispy. You may want to check one first however, just in case.

Cocktail Sauce

An all-too-common condiment throughout the States. Cocktail sauce is based on tomato ketchup (see below) and horseradish. It is always served with seafood in chain seafood restaurants, such as Long John Silver and The Red Lobster.

Chef Jimmy Schmidt, who is responsible for one of my favorite restaurants, The Rattlesnake Club in Detroit, has created a great recipe for cocktail sauce. Jimmy hated this notorious product so much that he completely re-invented it and even changed its name to Rooster Sauce. Jimmy uses roasted bell peppers. His mood inspired me. Using pickled green tomatoes in my Cocktail Sauce, makes for an interesting version, but make sure they are not just unripe red tomatoes.

3 cups (1¼ pints/750 ml) my ketchup or yours
½ cup (4 fl oz/125 ml) creamed horseradish
1 small white onion, grated
1 cup (5 oz/125 g) pickled green tomatoes
½ tbl soy sauce

1 tbl lemon juice
½ cup (2½ oz/60 g) parsley, finely chopped
1 tsp garlic salt
1 tsp black pepper, coarsely ground

Mix all ingredients thoroughly, remove air pockets by poking with a skewer. Bottle in preserving jars, and seal. Chill.

Tartar Sauce

Tartar Sauce is encountered as often as Cocktail Sauce and like Cocktail Sauce can be excellent, if properly prepared. It is usually served with fish, but tastes great with most white meats and, like Remoulade Sauce, it is a wonderful substitute for butter in sandwiches.

A key ingredient in Tartar Sauce is the pickle – cured cucumber. In Britain we are not that 'au fait' with this particular product, whereas in the States, they consume around 9 lb/4 kg a head per year. They have about 36 varieties and around 26 billion are packed annually.

Pickles come in three basic flavors – sweet, sour, and dill. The dill pickle and the kosher dill pickle are probably the most popular – the name referring to the dill herb used in the curing process. The term 'kosher' refers to the garlic added in the pickling process and has no religious connotation.

2 cups (16 fl oz/500 ml) mayonnaise, shop-
   bought is fine
1 sweet pickle, drained and finely diced
1 tbl green olives, diced
1 tbl shallots, diced
2 hard-boiled eggs, chopped
1 tbl capers

1 tbl chives, chopped
1 tsp dry mustard
1 tsp lemon juice
1 tbl fresh dill, chopped

Combine all the ingredients and refrigerate.

Thousand Island Dressing

Another much maligned sauce, and justifiably so, is Thousand Island Dressing. This one originated in the 1920s, probably in some bar in the Thousand Islands on the St Lawrence River, between New York and Ontario. I don't believe it has anything to do with the Pacific, as I have been told (one ingredient from each trading island). Again, I do not feel it's worth the effort to make your own mayonnaise, but use homemade ketchup for a good dressing.

1 cup (8 fl oz/250 ml) mayonnaise
1 cup (8 fl oz/250 ml) ketchup (see below)
1 medium white onion, grated
½ cup (2½ oz/60 g) olives, diced
1 small yellow bell pepper, diced small

½ cup (2½ oz/60 g) parsley, finely chopped
1 tsp Louisiana Hot Sauce
1 canned pimento, chopped
1 small red jalapeño, diced

Combine the ingredients and refrigerate.

Ketchup

Ketchup covers a variety of condiments, the most common being pickle and tomato. The Chinese invented the word 'ket-tsiap', meaning a pickled fish sauce. The F. and J. Heinz Co. of Pennsylvania first sold tomato ketchup in 1876. Since then most folk assume 'ketchup' is their brand, just as many Americans think ketchup is a vegetable.

I enjoy different ketchups – mushroom, banana, mango, and sweet pepper. The sauce is mainly used as a condiment but also serves as a short cut to other recipes, such as barbecue sauce or as an ingredient in meatloaf.

If you make your own ketchup – and I hope you do – be sure to remove any air which might cause discoloration. Similarly, once opened, oxidyzation can cause discoloration and darkening. The high acidity in ketchup, however, means it will not spoil easily, though once opened it should still be kept refrigerated.

At Kenny's we occasionally had exploding bottles of ketchup. Usually at the bar where the bartenders often neglected food chemistry, in favor of dispensing dreams.

10 tomatoes, skinned, cored and chopped
1 medium red onion, diced
1 medium red bell pepper, diced
1 tbl olive oil
1/2 cup (2 1/2 oz/60 g) raisins

1/2 cup (2 1/2 oz/60 g) brown sugar
1 orange, rind peeled and diced small
2 tbl red wine vinegar
1 tbl soy sauce
1 tsp Worcestershire Sauce

Sauté the tomato, onion and bell pepper for five minutes in the olive oil over high heat. Remove from heat and encourage the tomatoes to break. Add the rest of the ingredients, cool properly, and refrigerate. Check flavor after one hour.

Shrimp-Stuffed Jalapeños with Cheese

These are little green bombs created to wake up your palate and your general constitution. It is usually up to you how fiery they are. However, they have the propensity to fool you or make a fool of you. They look neat, and the cheese also helps to alleviate some of the heat. The shrimp tail is left sticking out of the pepper and the whole lot is breaded and fried. They come with many silly names, such as Texas Torpedoes and Scorpion Bites and are excellent as a party food, a garnish, or an appetizer.

You may find it wise to have a fruit salsa nearby and definitely some cold beer. (Actually dairy products are best for alleviating the pain created by chile peppers.)

Please do not feel you have to stay with my stuffing, as there are many ideas around, such as smoked chicken, lychees, or even try a vegetarian bean mix. You can vary the cheese or maybe try goat's cheese. Although I have to say Monterey Jack or a sharp Cheddar cheese is by far the best.

To reduce the chiles, heat a little, you may wish to follow a couple of steps - which become three on reflection.

1. Completely de-vein and de-seed the pepper. The vein is the white skin on the inside, mainly along the ribs of the pepper.
2. Soak the pepper in a water, vinegar, and salt solution for 30 minutes.
3. Boil the pepper in water for a few minutes - this will also make it easier to handle.

If you want all the heat, drop the chile in hot oil for a few minutes. Pull it out and cover with a towel, to sweat it. This will allow you to peel the chile, making it much easier to handle in this recipe. This is a convenient dish to prepare ahead of time to the chilling stage.

16 small, round, green jalapeños, treated as
  above
16 shrimp, peeled with tail left on
2 medium red onions, grated
6 tbl (3 oz/75 g) butter
2 tsp onion salt
2 tsp paprika

1 cup (5 oz/125 g) strong cheese, grated
2 eggs, beaten
1 cup (8 fl oz/250 ml) milk
1 cup (5 oz/125 g) dry breadcrumbs
2 tbl crushed pecans
About 1 cup (8 fl oz/250 ml) oil for frying

Halve the pepper, de-seed, and de-vein them. I usually split them down the center and use the larger side, keeping the smaller half for other uses; it is easier to stuff a rounded pepper. Sauté the onion in butter until soft then add seasonings. Let cool then add cheese.

Place the shrimp inside the jalapeño and push the cheese firmly around it, leaving the tail hanging out. Dip in batter. Combine the breadcrumbs and pecan nuts and roll the stuffed chiles in the breadcrumb mixture. Repeat. Chill until all are ready.

If you choose to serve them as a starter I find a Virgin Mary sauce a good accompaniment.

Virgin Mary Sauce

2 cups (16 fl oz/500 ml) V-8 juice
1 tsp Worcestershire Sauce
4 tsp lemon juice
2 tsp Louisiana Hot Sauce
2 tsp coarse-grained mustard

1 medium onion, halved and squeezed on lemon
  squeezer
1 tsp sea salt
2 tsp cayenne

Combine all the ingredients.

Buttermilk-Fried Softshell Crab with Lemon Butter and Pecan Rice

Chesapeake Bay is the largest bay in the world, with 4, 000 or so miles of shoreline. It produces a bounty of seafood, but the blue crab is by far the most important. The Bay provides more crabs for human consumption than any other body of water in the world. I have never been to see it, but Chesapeake Bay sounds like a real treasure trove for sea-foodies. It is situated on the Atlantic coast, flanked by Virginia and Maryland. Blue crabs favor the Bay because of the huge expanse of brackish water and bounty of food. But they are not the sole inhabitant of Chesapeake to be harvested – oysters, clams, and fish such as shad, are big news too.

The crabs, hard-shelled primarily, are harvested from early May to early October. During this period they will shed their skin to accommodate growth. In their three-year life span, providing no locals snag them with a big rake, they will molt up to 23 times. It is these moltings which are the basis of the U.S. softshell crab industry. The Bay accounts for 90% of the country's production.

The crabs are said to be best fresh. Makes sense huh? Well I don't know. When at the venerable Mr B's in New Orleans, I actually chose my own softshell from the walk-in. Exhilarating colors. But the final taste was no better than crabs frozen by experienced companies, such as J.T. Handy. (Handy has been in the frozen soft-shell crab business for 75 years, and each box still arrives with a personally signed card from the checking packer).

Soft-shell crabs are known under a banner of names – peelers, red signs, buster, back rams, sally crabs, and snots. However, despite the semantics, there is little debate when it comes to naming the grade sizes. They are:–

mediums   *3½ - 4-inch shell pan*
hotels   *4 - 4½-inch shell pan*

primes	*4½ - 5-inch shell pan*
jumbo's	*5 - 5½-inch shell pan*
whales	*5½ inches and over.*

The latter size is meant to be the largest commercial size, although I have been served 'slabs' (jumbo-sized) and the smallest I ever ate were not called 'mediums' but 'cocktails', and were almost certainly too small to be legal. Softshells are available at 'better' fishmongers in the UK. Trust me they are worth finding.

Softshells lend themselves to blackening and also smoking, both huge successes in my opinion. But best – fry them in buttermilk at exactly 375°F/190°C. You will have a beautiful sweet, crunchy delight.

If you cannot find buttermilk, combine milk with a dash of vinegar and leave for a few hours. Combine your buttermilk with lemon juice, sugar, and eggs. Season strong plain flour with paprika, garlic salt, and cayenne. You will obviously need oil for frying. Drop the crabs in the batter and ensure all the legs are splayed. Don't worry if one falls off, batter it, and replace when you arrange it on plates. No-one will notice. Dredge the battered crab in flour and shallow fry for 4-5 minutes; turn once. Drain and serve. Remind your guests to eat the whole crab, the 'funny' bits have been removed.

Pecan Rice

If you cannot find real pecan rice, don't worry. Just add a few drops each of soy sauce and Worcestershire Sauce to the boiling water when you cook regular long-grain rice.

1 medium white onion, grated
2 stalks celery, diced
2 tbl parsley, finely chopped
4 tbl (2 oz/50 g) unsalted butter
1 tsp garlic salt

1 tsp coarse-ground black pepper
1 small red jalapeño, finely diced
1 cup (5 oz/125 g) pecans, chopped
1 clove garlic, finely chopped
3 cups (1 1/2 lbs/750 g) cooked long-grain rice

Sauté onion, celery, and parsley in the butter; add the seasoning. Take off heat and add jalapeño and pecans. Mix with the cooked rice.

William H. Coleman in his 1885 *Guide* quotes a homesick Louisianian as saying, 'If I could get home and eat a dinner of soft-shell crabs and pompano once more, I'd be willing to eat blue beef all the rest of my life.' What the hell is 'blue beef'? But I guess you get the idea.

If you have never tried softshell crawfish, but feel like trying them (remember all crustaceans molt) do not bother. I wasted my money on them - and I guess you can learn from my lesson.

A rather decadent use for a softshell is in a sandwich. Outrageous. Sauté 1 tablespoon each of chopped chives, garlic, and grated red onion in 2 tbl (1 oz/25 g) butter and 4 tbl wine. Dredge the crab in flour then sauté for 5 minutes. Make a sandwich with ripe tomatoes, tartar sauce, and oakleaf lettuce. Of course use your most favorite bread. Enjoy.

Cornmeal-Fried Fish Sandwich

The frying of fish in cornmeal is very popular everywhere south of the Mason-Dixon Line, not just in Louisiana. I usually make this sandwich with catfish fillets, but it works real fine with any strong textured white fish, preferably a freshwater variety. Dredge the fillet in a simple batter and then in seasoned cornmeal. Only fry the fish for 4-5 minutes. Build a sandwich with Tartar sauce and truly ripe tomatoes. You can bet your friends will not have experienced it many times before.

Oyster Po' Boys

The Oyster Loaf in New Orleans is historically called 'la médiatrice' – the peacemaker. The story of la médiatrice is based around picaresque husbands who lingered a little too long in the bawdy French Quarter at night. On the way home, anticipating an earful from the wife, they would purchase an oyster loaf. (Oysters used to be ridiculously inexpensive.) The idea being that the sandwich would pacify a virago wife. Po' boys are now as much an integral part of the U.S. culinary psyche as submarines, hoagies, grinders, heroes, and other varieties of weird-shaped, jumbo-sized bread roll.

It is worth noting that you can no more explain an American sandwich to anyone outside the U.S. as you can explain cricket to an Eskimo, and despite my honest endeavors, I don't think the Oyster Loaf travels. New Orleans baguettes seem to be lighter and sweeter than anywhere else – as far as I am concerned.

A couple of alternatives I have enjoyed are the Po' Boy's Po' Boy, which is leftover roast potatoes, fried and covered in brown gravy and Shrimp Buster Po' Boy, a specialty from Herbie-K's in Shreveport, Louisiana where the tails hang out of each end. If I had to really choose what to eat forever it would be the Debris Po' Boy, found at the incomparable Mother's in New Orleans. There they soak the trimmings which fall off the roast beef in the meat juices, and pile it high. The worst Po' Boy – which I didn't taste – was at the Fatted Calf in New Orleans, peanut butter, bacon, and steak.

To me the original Cornmeal-Fried Oyster Po' Boy is still darling, closely followed by the Beer Batter Shrimp variety.

To make an Oyster Po' Boy, first assemble your filling. Slice your baguette in half and hollow out the bread. Toast it, then spread each side with Creole Mustard Dip (see p. 40). Cover one side with chopped tomatoes and the other with shredded lettuce. Fill with the main ingredient, combine, and enjoy.

Muffuletta

This is a sandwich particular to New Orleans, and shows the Sicilian influence on the city's cooking. I find muffulettas are best bought at the Central Grocery store on Decatur Street across from the French Market. This is a glorious emporium of exotic foodstuffs, freshly prepared and imported. The Napoleon House on Chartres Street does a mighty fine Muffuletta too.

The Muffuletta is a 10-inch/25 cm discus-shaped bun, covered in sesame seeds. The fillings in muffulettas are layers of corned beef, Genoa salami, and ham, plus layers of Provolone and Swiss cheese. All this plus an olive salad comprising marinated olives, garlic, cocktail onions, pimentos, capers, and more. You don't have to buy the whole loaf, fortunately. They are big.

'Peel 'n' Eat' Shrimp with Tequila Tomato Dipping Sauce

Serving up steaming bowls of unpeeled shrimp is as common in the States as moules marinière is in western Europe. It is great fun, takes pressure off the host, and is mighty fine eating. Just provide piles of napkins. I suggest you follow the recipe exactly on this occasion. The spicier the better is what I say.

Don't bother with this dish unless you have quality, raw shrimp or prawns, with their shells on. Make a 'boil' out of water, sliced onion, chopped parsley, lemon juice, cayenne, garlic salt, diced red jalapeños, and white wine. As soon as the stock is simmering, add the shrimp, turn them a few times and serve as soon as the shrimp have turned crimson.

If you have any shrimp left over, or you bought too many, save them for a shrimp salad. Just toss them with sweetcorn, cilantro (coriander), and julienned roast peppers.

Cajun Popcorn with Tequila-Tomato Dipping Sauce

This is one of the few marketing fads tied in to Louisiana cooking. It is a fun name, but in reality is nothing the rest of the world hasn't done at sometime or other. It simply consists of bite-sized pieces of a favorite food, dipped in a spicy batter, and fried. Like real popcorn (have you ever made it yourself? A real scream.) it is very 'moreish,' and will also make your guests drink much more than usual. Of course you may not want that.

3 cups (1 lb/450 g) meat, fish or eggplant
   (aubergine), cubed
1 cup (8 fl oz/250 ml) milk
2 eggs, beaten
½ (4 fl oz/125 ml) wine
1 tsp garlic salt
1 tsp paprika

1 tbl Louisiana Hot Sauce
2 cups (10 oz/250 g) plain flour
2 tsp cayenne
1 tsp coarse-ground black pepper
6 tbl parsley, finely chopped
2 cups (16 fl oz/500 ml) oil for deep frying

Choose your 'popcorn' meat(s), from crawfish tails, 'gator, chicken, shrimp bits, or eggplant cubes. Combine the milk, eggs, wine, garlic salt, paprika and hot sauce.

Make a seasoned flour by combining the flour with cayenne, black pepper, and finely chopped parsley. Double dredge, and deep fry. Serve immediately.

Tequila-Tomato Dipping Sauce

My father's birthday falls on Christmas Eve. We always closed early on this day to allow time for staff and family to come around for drinks. At one of these celebrations I prepared a meal for the gang. I was alone in the kitchen except for the most important guy in a restaurant – the potwash.

I was not in the best of moods due to this unexpected situation. Consequently, I 'knocked up' a series of dishes, taking as many short cuts as possible. One dish was Sautéed Alligator with a Tomato-Tequila Sauce. To my amazement, the crowd went wild.

All I did was cook some homemade ketchup with tequila, white wine, creamed horseradish, scallions and seasoning. (I had tequila in the kitchen for 'sousing,' shrimp in case you were wondering – I never drink at work.) Duncan, one of the bartenders, in particular, went crazy for the sauce, 'the best sauce ever.' I didn't have the heart to tell him I had just used up what was nearest, no reducing or stock-making, or any type of prep at all. But give it a go, you may be surprised, I certainly was.

½ cup (4 fl oz/125 ml) silver tequila
1 cup ketchup, preferably homemade (p. 101)
½ cup (4 fl oz/125 ml) white wine
1 cup (5 oz/125 g) scallions (spring onions),
   chopped

1 tbl creamed horseradish
1 tsp garlic salt
1 tsp ground white pepper
1 tsp paprika

Combine all ingredients and chill. Slightly warm up for service, this will bring extra flavors out from the horseradish and onion.

Beer-Batter Coconut Shrimp with Honey-Mustard Dip

In Britain, we have known coconuts for many years, at least since the 1550s. In the tropics, they had cottoned on to their uses much earlier. I ask, why bother with fresh coconut? Okay, I know the milk is refreshing, the flesh, when mashed into another form of milk, useful, and it generally has many other culinary uses. But to me, it is just a pain. Go to the store and buy a box of desiccated coconut. No hammers, mess, lost time, or hairy bits. Fruit of paradise? Fruit of pain in the ass to me.

1 cup (8 fl oz/250 ml) strong beer
2 eggs, beaten
2 cups (10 oz/250 g) plain flour
20 large raw shrimp
1 tsp garlic salt

1 tsp cayenne
1 cup (5 oz/125 g) desiccated coconut
2 tbl parsley, finely chopped
2 lettuces, leaves separated and tossed in
   dressing

Make a beer batter out of strong beer, beaten eggs, and flour. Peel the shrimp but leave on the tail. Butterfly the shrimp and pull out the dark vein. Sprinkle shrimp with garlic salt and cayenne. Dip each shrimp in batter, then roll in desiccated coconut, to which you have added the parsley. Set aside. Make sure you pressed coconut into the back of shrimp, this way they will curl when frying and sit up pretty on the plate for you. Smother the honey-mustard dip around the plate, place a small ball of dressed lettuces in the middle, and surround with shrimp. Allow about five shrimp to a portion. Don't provide cutlery.

Honey Mustard Dip

1 cup (8 fl oz/250 ml) coarse-grained mustard
1 tbl cider vinegar
1 tbl olive oil
1 tbl honey or golden syrup, at room temperature

1 tbl lemon juice
½ cup (4 fl oz/125 ml) orange juice
1 tbl parsley, finely chopped
1 tsp onion salt

Combine all ingredients. Keep at room temperature until you are ready to serve it.

Crabmeat Cheesecake with White Wine Broth

A couple of years back, I traveled through Alabama to meet up with some buddies in New Orleans. This happened to be at the same time as the First Annual Gulf of Mexico Seafood Culinary Competition was in progress. The competing Louisiana team produced an inspired dish, now copied everywhere. It was a crabmeat cheesecake with a crab cream sauce. I borrowed the idea and have since played around with it, my smoked salmon cheesecake proving a great success at Sunday brunch.

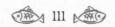

3 cups (1 lb/450 g) crabmeat, white and brown meat
1 medium white onion, grated
1 small red jalapeño, diced real small
4 tbl (2 oz/50 g) butter
1 tsp sea salt
1 tsp ground white pepper
2 eggs, beaten
½ cup (2½ oz/60 g) smoked salmon, chopped
1 cup (5 oz/125 g) cream cheese, at room temperature for easier mixing
4 tbl parsley, finely chopped

2 tbl fresh dill, finely chopped
2 tbl chives, finely chopped

White wine broth
2 scallions (spring onions), finely chopped
2 tbl (1 oz/25 g) butter
½ tsp sea salt
½ tsp coarse-ground black pepper
1 cup (8 fl oz/250 ml) white wine
1 yellow bell pepper, finely chopped
1 red jalapeño, finely diced

Briefly sauté onion and jalapeño in butter. Take them off the heat and add sea salt and pepper. Combine the cheese, eggs, salmon, and crab. Don't mix too hard. Add cooled onion mix. Butter a shallow baking dish and spread mixture over to a thickness of about 2 in/10 cm. Bake at 275°F/140°C for 15 minutes.

To serve, portion into ramekins or dariole molds, let set (this only takes 5 minutes), and invert onto a plate. Remove ramekin and broil under a hot grill for 2-3 minutes. Then smother with the white wine broth. We don't want the cheesecake too hot, as this will kill the flavors. Garnish with a combination of finely chopped parsley, dill, and chives. Sprinkle with paprika.

For the white wine broth - sauté chopped scallions in butter, add seasoning, add wine, and reduce. Add yellow bell pepper and red jalapeño. Double again with wine and bring to simmer then serve.

CHICKEN AND FRIENDS

BEANS

Barbecuing with Kenny

Most of my favorite restaurants offer 'down-home' styles of cooking. It is often here we find the service your Mom would be proud of. Barbecue shacks are such places.

Barbecue is – after the revered fried chicken – the most important cooking style to the American populace. It is shrouded in mystery and given serious treatment. The word evokes images of obscure, dark shacks, full of smoky hazes, crusty jugs of various sauces, and aging pit-masters.

Recipes and preparation techniques vary from region to region, neighborhood to neighborhood, even brother to brother. Unless, that is, your nearest BBQ restaurant is part of a national chain – Heaven forbid!

In Tennessee, they put all the emphasis on the sauce, in Carolina sauce is no big deal. In Knoxville they slice their meat, but over in Memphis it is chopped. In Owensboro, Kentucky, mutton is the preferred meat, in South Georgia, it is goat. In Richmond, Virginia, they prefer pork butt, coarsely chopped. (By the way this is not the ass of the pig, but where the pork shoulder butts up against the torso.)

To add to this confusion there are three distinctive types of seasoning and sauces that are used.

a) Dry seasonings rubbed onto the meat before grilling.

b) Marinades and basting sauces are used before and during cooking.

c) Sauces are brushed onto the meat just before the meat is done, then served at the table as a condiment.

The name 'barbecue' comes from the Spanish and Haitian-Creole word 'barbacoa,' meaning a framework of sticks. It refers to a kind of grill on which meat was roasted. Today it has a wider meaning – social gatherings and different ways of cooking. It does have one significant requirement, in my opinion, – a sauce. The BBQ sauce.

I have never been or wanted to go to Texas but, I am told, in the Lone Star State, beef is the norm. Cooked over hickory or oak and without a sauce – dry barbecue. I strongly disagree with the dry method, especially for home cooking. You will see why.

According to Ed Powers of the G.A. Pit outside Brunswick, Georgia, 'to ask a barbecue man to tell you his sauce recipe is like asking to borrow his wife.' Get the drift?

I developed my recipe after playing with various styles (plus a lot of TLC). I suggest you choose a style which you like and develop it. For example, in the eastern part of North Carolina they use a sauce style enjoyed by George Washington, combining cider vinegar, sugar, salt, and cayenne. In North Carolina, over the division line of U.S. Route 1, they turn the same sauce red, using ketchup, and this is occasionally referred to as the Lexington Sauce. However, in South Carolina, the color turns yellow, as they drown it in mustard.

Down in Georgia they use equal quantities of mustard and ketchup. This creates a sweeter flavor, much preferred in the Southern regions. Over in Texas, if there is a sauce, it has to be much stronger to combat the strong flavor of their beef and the longer cooking times required. This necessitates the introduction of heavy spicing. I don't really agree with the introduction of Tabasco, as it burns off too quickly and would suggest you use more ground red pepper pods.

Probably the best-known barbecue city is Kansas City. Up there, BBQ is a religion. Even in the television sit-com 'MASH' they refer to it in hallowed tones. Kansas City recipes are the styles I prefer. Sort of combining the best of the rest.

House Barbecue Sauce

1 cup (8 fl oz/250 ml) chicken stock
2 cups (16 fl oz/500 ml) ketchup
1 cup (5 oz/125 g) brown sugar
1 tbl Louisiana Hot Sauce
1 tbl soy sauce
1 tbl Worcestershire Sauce
1 medium red onion, grated (release those
    juices)

1 tsp garlic salt
1 tsp garlic powder
1 tsp paprika
2 tsp cayenne
1 tbl red wine vinegar
1 tsp liquid smoke (optional)

Combine all in a saucepan and cook slowly for 20 minutes, covered. I actually use a double boiler but you may find this a little boring.

Barbecue Spice Mix

1 tsp onion powder
1 tbl garlic powder
1 tsp oregano, dried
1 tsp thyme, dried

1 tbl paprika
1 tbl cayenne
1 tsp chili powder
1 tsp cinnamon

Barbecue Rub

3 tbl garlic salt
2 tbl ground black pepper
2 tbl paprika
2 tbl white sugar

2 tbl red pepper flakes
1 tbl onion powder
1 tbl chili powder
2 tsp mustard powder

Barbecued Chicken

2-3 lb/1 kg chicken, cut into tenths (p. 238)
About 1 cup (8 fl oz/250 ml) olive oil
4 tbl red pepper flakes.

3 cups (1¼ pints/750 ml) House Barbecue Sauce
  (p. 116)

SERVES 4-6

A simple delight. Brush the chicken pieces with oil, let drain, and sprinkle with red pepper flakes. Coat each chicken piece with the Barbecue Sauce and then roast at 400°F/200°C/gas mark 6, skin side up. Turn chicken after 20 minutes, then again every 5 minutes for 20 minutes. Do not pierce the meat, as you may lose valuable juices. The juices can also cause a flare up.

Keep basting while turning, then after 20 minutes, remove from oven and see how it's doing. It should be nearly cooked. We need this break to slow down the cooking, because this will ultimately lead to a juicier bird. Re-coat the chicken with BBQ sauce and finish off under the grill. This could take another 20 minutes, so keep the heat low. A grilled outer skin gives a nicer finish, together with contributing even more flavors.

You may wish to leave the chicken in the sauce overnight for a stronger flavor.

Barbecued Salmon

Okay, I know this should be in the fish section and the following in meats, but give me a break.

2 8 oz/250 g wild salmon fillets, I know you
  wouldn't use farmed
½ cup (4 fl oz/125 ml) olive oil
1 tsp Barbecue Rub (p. 116)
2 tbl (1 oz/25 g) butter
1 medium white onion

1 tsp Barbecue Spice Mix (p. 116)
1 tsp soy sauce
1 tsp hot sauce
3 cups (1 lb/450 g) cooked sweetcorn
3 cups (1 lb/450 g) cooked red kidney beans

Brush fillets with olive oil. Rub fish with BBQ Rub and broil for 10 minutes maximum. Meanwhile, warm the butter and grate the onion into it; sauté for 3 minutes. Add spice mix and sauces. Cook for 3 minutes over high heat. Remove the salmon, arrange it on serving plates, pour the sauce over it, and serve with sweetcorn and red kidney beans.

Barbecued Baby Back Ribs

This is rather the definitive recipe. I've not held back, even though some ingredients may be difficult to find. Just remember these recipes can be adapted to any meats.

20 lb/12 kg baby back ribs
4 cloves garlic, finely chopped
6 tbl (3 oz/75 g) unsalted butter
2 tsp ground black pepper
2 cups (16 fl oz/500 ml) Hot Sauce (p. 18)
2 cups (16 fl oz/500 ml) House BBQ Sauce
   (p. 116)

2 cups (16 fl oz/500 ml) beef stock
1/2 cup (4 fl oz/125 ml) lemon juice
1 tbl Worcestershire Sauce
1 tbl soy sauce
1 tbl liquid smoke (p. 238)
1/2 cup (4 oz/125 g) white onion, diced
2 cups (8 oz/250 g) Barbecue Spice Mix (p. 116)

SERVES 10-12

Sauté onion and garlic in butter. Combine with the pepper, Sauce, beef stock, lemon juice, Worcestershire and soy sauces, and the liquid smoke. Add to the diced onion, and remove from heat as soon as they reach a simmer. Stir well then slowly cook for 30 minutes. Lightly brush ribs with Barbecue Spice Mix and bake at 275°F/140°C/gas mark 1 for two hours. Remove from oven and brush well with sauce, cook for a further 20 minutes. Broil under a high heat. Depending on your taste, you may wish to brush the ribs again. Serve as soon as the edges are charring.

Serve the spare sauce hot on the side, for your friends to add if they feel the need. Just don't waste it.

Fried Chicken

'You take a chicken and you kill it
and you put it in a skillet
You fry it to a golden brown
that's southern cooking
and it's mighty fine.'

Ernestine Mills

If you cook fried chicken at home, everyone will love you. Don't be scared off by the fact that everyone who cooks it claims theirs is the best. It is just that one cook's best is very different from the next cook's.

My favorite restaurant in the whole wide world for fried chicken is sadly no longer with us – Chez Helene in New Orleans. Chef Austin Leslie is probably the finest interpreter of this dish anywhere and, despite the restaurant's remote location, it was always packed. Southern divorce lawyers sat beside Southern housewives, sat beside Southern beatniks, sat beside me.

This leaves the Hummingbird Café, also in New Orleans, as my current favorite fried chicken joint. Great juke box, packed with taxi drivers and dying hippies. It's wonderful. Tom Waits would sing about it, Charles Bukowski would write about it, and Robert Altman would make a movie about it. It was here, at the Hummingbird, that I first learned to prepare fried chicken. For me, even at 1.30 a.m. with a bucket of Dixie Beer and Jack Daniels swilling about inside me, it was an *exemplary cooking lesson*.

Kenny's Fried Chicken

We have to do three preps here – batter, flour, and the chicken.

2-3 lb/1 kg chicken, cut into tenths (see p. 238)
3 tsps paprika
3 tsp coarse-ground black pepper
3 tsp garlic salt
3 tsp white pepper

1½ cups (8 oz/200 g) plain flour
1¼ pint (10 fl oz/300 ml) milk, full-cream milk,
   or single cream
1 egg, beaten
About 2 cups (16 fl oz/500 ml) groundnut oil

In a large mixing bowl combine 2 tsps each of paprika, black pepper, garlic salt, and ground white pepper. I assume their are no lumps. Drop each chicken piece into the seasoning and coat. You may find it easier to do this in a paper bag, just shake it. Place the seasoned chicken in the refrigerator. Whilst it is chilling, add the remaining seasoning to the flour. Set aside.

In another large mixing bowl combine the milk (or full-cream milk or single cream) with one beaten egg. Mix together. Retrieve the chicken. Fancy a beer? Let the chicken reach room temperature, the flavors wake up. You will now need a deep strong frying pan, enough to hold 2-3 inches/5-7 cm of groundnut oil. Pre-heat oil to around 350°F/180°C. Whilst it is warming up, let your household buddies know of its existence.

Dip the chicken into the flour, into the batter and back into the flour. The key here is to have one hand for 'dry' and the other for 'wet.' Then start frying, adding meatiest parts first, they will take longest to cook. Do not crowd the pieces. If you start to have some popping, don't worry, unless it becomes very loud, just take the pan off the heat for a while. You may have realized by now that is sensible to roll your sleeves down. My apologies if it's too late. Also keep the handle of the frying pan facing inwards.

We are aiming for a crispy batter and a juicy, fully cooked bird. It will take 20 minutes or so for the thick leg and thigh pieces, about 12-15 minutes for the wings and smaller breast pieces. This I first learnt at the Hummingbird, unfortunately it meant more beers and putting more quarters in the juke-box. All good fun!

Every few minutes, carefully turn the chicken - tongs are best. Resist the temptation to raise or lower the heat, unless you are in trouble. You will know when your chicken is cooked by the appearance of exposed bones, less popping and general know-how. Remove from the pan and let cool, no patting with kitchen towels please.

Unless you serve the chicken pieces straight away - I'd reckon they are a little too hot, yes? - place them on a baking tray and put them in the oven, at a low temperature. This will also ensure they are fully cooked.

If you are worried about having hot oil around for so long or you need the cooking space, steal my restaurant trick. Quickly fry the chicken pieces until the batter is crispy, about 5 minutes, then transfer to a baking tray and bake for 30 minutes or so at 375°F/190°C/gas mark 5. This is easy and safe, especially if you are making a large batch, although the flavor is not quite the same. Whatever, it is still mighty fine eating. Enjoy.

Don't waste the residual frying oil. Pour off the majority of it, then reheat the pan. No doubt it will be full of crumbs. Add enough flour to soak up whatever oil is left. Mix in thoroughly, add seasoning, and serve with your fried chicken. This is called Saw Mill Gravy down Louisiana way.

A platter of fried chicken is perfect for the dinner table, allowing everyone to help themselves, if and when they want. You can also show off by covering the table in colorful and interesting side-dishes. Here are a few of my favorites.

Sweet Potatoes

What is the difference between a sweet potato and a yam, a question I am frequently asked. The sweet potato is a yellow-orange tuber and grows on vines. It is native to the New World tropics. There are two dominant types, the pale 'sweet potato' and the darker, fleshy type, erroneously called 'yams.' The true yam is a different tropical vine, sweeter and much bigger. A much rarer sight. There you have it, as clear as the shrimp-prawn issue.

Candied Yams

This dish is too sweet for me, but has a gorgeous smell whilst cooking. When added to a large holiday platter it contributes a new taste dimension – for sure.

2 large sweet potatoes, cut into big pieces and
    parboiled for 10 minutes
1 cup (8 fl oz/250 ml) water
1 cup (5 oz/125 g) dark brown sugar
Pinch of nutmeg

Pinch of cinnamon
2 oranges, coarsely chopped; don't lose any juice
1 small white onion, diced
Butter

Bring the water, sugar, and seasonings to boil. Combine the potatoes with the oranges and onion, then add to the pot. Keep boiling until the liquid is reduced to half. Remove contents with a slotted spoon and transfer to a baking dish and dot with butter. Reduce liquid a little more then pour into dish. Bake at 275°F/140°C/gas mark 1 for 45 minutes or until sticky. You may need to stir a couple of times.

To adapt the Candied Yam recipe, omit the cinnamon and half the sugar. Add a cup (5 oz/125 g) of chopped pecans and a huge shot of brandy and you will have - Sweet Potato Pecan Casserole.

Sweet Potato Fries

The term 'French fry' has nothing to do with France, where they are called 'pommes frites.' Instead, it refers to a method called 'frenching,' which means cutting the potatoes into narrow strips. The Oxford Dictionary traces French fried potatoes back to 1894 and suggests it is an American term.

Anyway, at Kenny's, sweet potato fries sold roughly half as well as regular fries. I called the regular fries 'French Quarter Fries,' after the Vieux Carré in New Orleans. Both types were given a healthy coating of garlic salt, paprika, and cayenne. If you find your guests don't like this seasoning, apologize, and eat them yourself. You can 'fry' the seasoning off, but it will mess up your oil, as salt breaks the oil down and ruins its performance.

For a fancy version of sweet potato fries – make an egg-milk batter like others in this book but including crushed pecans and chicken-fry them (see Chicken-Fried Steak, p. 163). It is also fun to make Buttermilk Chicken-fried French Fries or you can even cook pickles this way, just make them spicy.

Succotash

Remember the Warner Brothers cartoons? When Yosemite Sam – the short, angry, pistol-packer with the orange moustache – says 'suffering succotash!' I bet you never knew what he was talking about. Right? Now you do, he was referring to a cooked dish of corn and beans, preferably lima (broad) beans.

It is a very Southern dish, though also eaten in New Mexico where the roadrunner is the State bird. The term is an Americanism, formed from the Narrangansett Indian word 'misickquatash.' There is no exact recipe. One version I sampled was a ham and succotash stew with Cheddar-flavored American biscuits (a sort of scone.) The chef presented it as a main course – it was excellent.

3 sweetcorn cobs
1 large white onion, sliced
1 cup (5 oz/125 g) smoked ham, coarsely chopped
4 tbl (2 oz/50 g) butter
2 tsp Cajun seasoning
½ cup (4 fl oz/125 ml) white wine or stock
  (optional)

1 cup (5 oz/125 g) lima (broad) beans (cooked
  fresh are best)
1 medium yellow bell pepper, diced fine
1 small red jalapeño, diced very small
Snipped chives to garnish

Slice the corn kernels from the cobs, keep juice and cobs for stock. Sauté the onion and ham in the butter for a few minutes. Add corn, beans, and seasoning, sauté for 3 minutes. You may need a little wine or stock to loosen the mixture.

After 10 minutes add yellow bell pepper and jalapeño, they add flavor, but, more importantly, color. Take off heat. Garnish with chives.

I like to add ham, but many recipes do not call for it, similarly some folk add cream. I don't feel succotash should have it, but it's up to you. Chives are a nice garnish, although parsley chopped fine works just as well. If you leave the ham out and substitute avocado at the bell pepper stage, you have another side-order or salad, maybe add some shrimp. You'll have to come up with your own name, however.

Macquechoux

Whereas succotash fluctuates from vegetarian and back, macquechoux (mack-SHOO) has no dead animals anywhere near it. It is a Cajun dish based, once again, on corn. That is all I know about it, but it makes a wonderful colorful and aromatic side-order. All the ingredients have to be fresh or you may come out with a Cajun equivalent of the English nightmare – Bubble and Squeak.

You can save the corn cobs to make a stock, perhaps for a Crab and Corn bisque or as an addition to Creamed Corn.

6 tbl (3 oz/75 g) butter

2 cups (10 oz/250 g) fresh corn kernels

1 small red jalapeño, diced small

1 tsp Cajun seasoning (p. 19)

1/2 cup (4 fl oz/125 ml) white wine

1 cup (5 oz/125 g) tomatoes, skinned, cored, and diced

33 scallions (spring onions), diced, for garnish

FOR THE TRINITY

1 cup (5 oz/125 g) green bell pepper, coarsely chopped

1 cup (5 oz/125 g) celery, coarsely chopped

1 cup (5 oz/125 g) white onion, coarsely chopped

Melt butter and sauté trinity until onion is soft. Remove with a slotted spoon and add corn and jalapeño. Sauté for 5 minutes or until corn begins to brown. Add seasonings, wine and tomato. As soon as pan begins to simmer, replace trinity. Serve as soon as pan is dry. Garnish with scallions.

Creamed Corn

A simple side-dish, but one found on many dinner tables at home. The intrinsic strength of the corn's flavor allows you to play with other interwoven flavors.

2 cups (10 oz/250 g) corn kernels

1 medium white onion, grated

1 medium red jalapeño, diced fine

6 tbl (2 1/2 oz/60 g) butter

1 tsp soy sauce

2 tbl double cream

4 tbl parsley, finely chopped

2 scallions (spring onions), diced

Sauté onion and jalapeño in butter, after five minutes add corn and soy sauce. Cook for five minutes add cream, parsley, and scallions. Serve two minutes later.

White Beans 'that make you crazy'

I used to call this dish simply White Beans, but after the tenth time of burning the dish I renamed it. For some reason, white beans stick to my pan more than any other type. But, they are wonderful and can be served at any time – with grilled andouille sausage for lunch, or topped with eggs for brunch. You may wish to call them 'crazy' because they taste so good. White beans or butter beans are called 'statewides' at Merle's Grill, Shreveport, Louisiana.

3 cups (1 lb/450 g) white or butter beans
1 tsp garlic salt
1 cup (5 oz/125 g) smoked ham, diced from
  preferably a smoked ham hock
6 tbl (3 oz/75 g) butter
1 cup (8 fl oz/250 fl oz) chicken stock
1 tbl Cajun seasoning (p. 19)
1 tbl White Roux (p. 21)
2 scallions chopped (optional)

1 tsp paprika (optional)

FOR THE TRINITY

½ cup (2½ oz/60 g) green bell pepper, coarsely
  chopped
½ cup (2½ oz/60 g) celery, coarsely chopped
½ cup (2½ oz/60 g) white onion, coarsely
  chopped

Soak the beans overnight and cook them in fresh water to cover for 2 hours. Discard water and set aside.

Sauté trinity with garlic salt and ham for ten minutes. Bring chicken stock to boil with Cajun seasoning. Add beans and trinity, cook for one hour. Add roux and check for 'sticking.' Cook for a further 60 minutes. Stir well and keep lid on until needed.

Scallions and a sprinkle of paprika are good to garnish with.

To convert this into Creole White Bean Soup, just mix in 2 cups (16 fl oz/500 ml) tomato soup at the end. Keep it loose.

'Drunken' Green Beans

Having renamed the white beans I felt obliged to rename the green beans.

I sauté these green beans in Pernod (the biggest-selling branded liquor in the world) or Herbsaint, or Ricard. I decided to call them 'drunken,' after the pourer fell out of the bottle neck! Normally, the booze flavor is mild and doesn't linger. I use French or haricot beans, but other beans – pole or snap beans – work fine, just play with cooking times.

1 medium white onion, diced
2 tbl (1 oz/25 g) butter
2 cloves garlic, finely chopped
3 cups (1 lb/450 g) green haricot beans, trimmed

1 tsp Ricard
1 cup (8 fl oz/250 ml) white wine
1 tsp sea salt

Sauté onion in butter and after a few minutes add garlic; allow to soften. Add Ricard and wine bring to a simmer then add beans and sea salt. Cover and serve as soon as the liquid has evaporated.

Squash Delight

Easy home cooking, Cajun-style.

3 cups (1 lb/450 g) yellow squash, sliced and
    boiled until tender
1/2 cup (5 oz/125 g) Cheddar cheese, grated
1 tsp ground white pepper
1 tsp sea salt
1 cup (5 oz/125 g) pecans, chopped coarsely
1/2 cup (4 fl oz/125 ml) mayonnaise

4 tbl seasoned breadcrumbs for topping

FOR THE TRINITY

1/2 cup (2 1/2 oz/60 g) red bell pepper, coarsely
    chopped
1/2 cup (2 1/2 oz/60 g) celery, coarsely chopped
1/2 cup (2 1/2 oz/60 g) onion, coarsely chopped

Slice the squash and boil it until tender. Sauté trinity, let cool. Combine the Cheddar cheese with the pepper and salt. Mix with the other ingredients and place in a greased baking dish. Top with breadcrumbs and bake at 325°F/170°C/gas mark 3 for 45 minutes.

Guacamole

I imagine most folk have an idea what this buttery dip is. Guacamole does not really belong to the South, but who cares?

3 large avocados

4 large tomatoes, firm, ripe and not beefsteak

1 medium white onion, grated

2 medium green chiles, chopped fine

½ cup (2½ oz/60 g) cilantro (coriander),
   coarsely chopped

2 tbl lemon or lime juice

1 cloves garlic, finely chopped

1 tsp garlic salt

1 tsp cayenne

Chop the tomatoes finely. Take the flesh from the avocados and mash. Do this just before serving and don't use a metallic implement. Combine tomatoes and avocados with all the rest of the ingredients. Enjoy.

If you prefer your guacamole creamier, be real Southern and cheat by adding sour cream or mayonnaise. I pass on that tip, my buddy from Fayetteville swears by it.

Roasting a Bird

Despite becoming really very bored preparing roast chicken (we roasted dozens a day for use in jambalaya and etouffée and for bones needed in stock, and for staff sandwiches), I still consider a golden-brown, roasted chicken a wonderful sight, with its succulent, moist meat and crispy golden skin.

I always season the bird inside and outside with lemon juice and garlic salt, then roast it breast down for 25 minutes. I take it out and add more seasoning, onion, and water to the roasting dish and then rub butter over the breasts, and maybe sprinkle on a little more garlic salt. Throughout the roasting, keep basting and adding more butter, along with juicing the bird it helps with the gravy. A 3 lb/1 kg bird should take 1 hour 15 minutes in a 425°F/220°C/gas mark 7 preheated oven. When you have taken the bird out of the oven, try and leave it for 10 minutes or so before carving, it will hold together better.

To make a gravy just mix in a little cream and use whatever seasonings are your favorite, maybe try soy sauce. If the gravy remains a little 'greesy', firstly swear at the god of chicken farmers and mix in a little sifted flour.

I rarely stuff my birds, preferring to make a dressing, and I cook this separately from the bird, but in the same oven. When I do stuff a bird, I like to use a herb stuffing with bacon, brown mushrooms, and oatmeal. Manna.

Herb Stuffing Recipe

1 medium white onion, sliced
2 scallions (spring onions), chopped
6 rashers streaky bacon, diced and fried
2 cups (8 oz/250 g) brown mushrooms, halved

1 cup (4 oz/125 g) medium oatmeal
1 tsp garlic salt
2 tsp ground white pepper
1 tbl parsley, finely chopped

Combine all the ingredients.

Some of my other favorite stuffings are, mashed potato and apple, cornbread, sausage and scallion, mushrooms, walnut and rosemary; or couscous, raisin, jalapeño and chive.

Chicken Fricassée

Chicken fricassée is a tradition in Cajun country. (Yes, you are correct, they have a fair few.) It is a dish of stewed or fried meat in a white sauce. On the one rare occasion when I had some extra fried chicken, I attempted the dish – it was a winner. To the Cajuns, cooking and eating come a very close second to having fun. I don't think there is a third. Fricassée is an economical meal, which cooks with very little supervision.

I was going to adapt a version of Mrs Kiley-Sandford's recipe for fricasséed duck breast, from her recipe published by The Junior League of Baton Rouge in 1959. For some reason, I could not produce anything like a fricassée. Mrs Sandford, please open a restaurant or come over here. I need to experience your cooking.

Anyway, here is my recipe and I know it works. It will serve between 4 and 6. Basically, you are browning a floured chicken, removing it from the pan, making a rich sauce with the gravy, replacing the chicken, and cooking it 'down easy.' Here goes … by the way, it is really a traditional French style of cooking.

2-3 lb/1 kg chicken, cut into 10 pieces (p. 238)
1½ cups (8 oz/200 g) plain flour
6 tbl (3 oz/75 g) butter
½ cup (2½ oz/60 g) shallots, diced
1 cup (8 fl oz/250 ml) chicken stock
1 tsp garlic salt

1 tsp ground white pepper
pinch of cumin
1 cup (5 oz/125 g) mushrooms, chopped fine
1 cup (8 fl oz/250 ml) white wine
½ cup (4 fl oz/125 ml) double cream
1 tbl parsley, finely chopped

Warm butter. Roll chicken in flour and brown in butter. Add shallots, keep cooking and loosening with stock. Add salt, pepper, and cumin, after 15 minutes add mushrooms, wine and top with stock. Bring to simmer and add cream and parsley. Cook out for further 10 minutes or until chicken is cooked. Serve over buttered noodles, rice, or mashed potatoes.

Chicken Pontalba

Occasionally I enjoy fancy food, but not often, and usually for ulterior motives. This dish is nice, and not too tricky.

In Chicken Pontalba, vegetables and lean ham are sautéed in butter and sit under a layer of crispy vegetables, on top of which we place a lightly grilled chicken breast. Finally, we smother the chicken, traditionally with Bearnaise but, as I loathe tarragon – I think we all need pet hates ('she says there are ants in the carpet') – I use a customized Hollandaise sauce.

As this recipe is rather fancy I have developed Rima and Richard Collins' recipe from the highly acclaimed *New Orleans Cookbook* (published by Knopf 1975) but produced one which is a little more workable.

I have read recipes for Pontalba which direct the cook to deep-fry the chicken and deep-fry the potatoes. Not for me. Either grill or broil the chicken after rubbing it with olive oil and then seasoning. Guinea fowl works even better for this recipe, but then again it does for most chicken recipes, unless you have a top grade chicken.

1 2-3 lb/1 kg chicken, cut into tenths (p. 238)

1 cup (5 oz/125 g) mushrooms, coarsely chopped

1 medium white onion, finely chopped

4 scallions (spring onions), finely chopped

4 tbl (2 oz/50 g) butter

4 rashers streaky bacon, diced and fried

3 medium potatoes, cut into regular sized small cubes

1 small red jalapeño

2 cloves garlic, finely chopped

½ cup (4 fl oz/125 ml) stock (optional)

1 cup (8 fl oz/250 ml) white wine

1 tbl soy sauce

1 tsp garlic salt

1 tsp ground white pepper

4 tbl olive oil

1 tsp coarse-ground black pepper

1 tsp sea salt

1 tbl parsley, finely chopped

2 cups (16 fl oz/500 ml) Hollandaise sauce (p. 99), mixed with 1 tsp tomato, diced and mixed fresh herbs (just don't serve me Bearnaise)

Sauté mushrooms and onions in butter and bacon for 5-10 minutes, remove and add potatoes, jalapeño and garlic. Stir well then cook for another 10 minutes. You may need a little stock to stop sticking. Remove from heat, add wine, soy, and seasoning. Rub chicken in oil, then sea salt and coarse ground black pepper and parsley. Broil until skin is crispy. Place pan back on heat and bring to simmer. Pour the sauce onto a plate, top with chicken, and smother in Hollandaise. Enjoy.

Yeasty Rolls

Serve these every time you sit down for dinner, timing it so they leave the oven just as y'all sit down. Also play with the flavors. I have enjoyed making cheese, diced black olive, crispy bacon, and cheese rolls. My favorite version, though, was Green Jalapeño Yeasty Rolls.

5 cups (1 ½ lb/1.25 kg) strong plain flour
2 tsp salt
2 tsp dry yeast

4 tbl olive oil
2 cups (16 fl oz/500 ml) warm water

Mix together the flour, salt, and yeast in a large bowl. If you adding anything funky do it now. Stir oil into warm water and add to flour. Knead together until your arms ache and the dough is smooth, about 8 minutes. Place dough back in bowl and cover with oiled clingfilm. Place the bowl somewhere warm and leave for at least an hour.

Knead dough for 2 minutes. I suggest you just count to 120 as you are doing this, rather than pretending to time yourself, you will only get it wrong. Cut dough into 18 'roll' shapes, place on a greased tray, touching each other. Cover again and leave somewhere warm for 20 minutes. Heat oven to 425°F/220°C/gas mark 7 and bake for 15 minutes. Enjoy.

Kenny's Hot Wings

Buffalo chicken wings originated at the Anchor Bar in Buffalo, upstate New York in either 1964 or 1969. Authenticity depends on who you believe. Either the bar's owner Frank Bellisimo, who says '69 and that they originated by the butcher screwing up, or his son Dom. Dom will regale you with a tale from '64, when some devout Roman Catholics craved some non-fishy food on the stroke of Friday midnight. Both versions do agree on one point – Mrs Teressa Bellisimo prepared them.

The wings should be deep fried (aaargh!), drowned in red-hot pepper sauce, and served with a blue cheese dressing and celery. I imagine celery was on the bar for Bloody Marys and became written into the scene by chance. Please do not fry your wings. It is disgusting. They do not need a dip, that goes without saying.

I suggest you mix up a marinade/baste. Keep the wings in it for a few hours, then bake. Let them cool after cooking, try a few, then grill them over or under a high heat and serve. They will be excellent, and you will probably find you have not made enough. An outdoor grill is best, this way you have the extra smoky flavor. (Always cut off the ugly wingtips.) Patently, this is not the original method, so call them after your home town – Altoona Chicken Wings perhaps.

½ cup (4 fl oz/125 ml) Louisiana Hot Sauce (p. 18)

⅓ cup (2½ fl oz/80 ml) Worcestershire Sauce

⅓ cup (2½ fl oz/80 ml) soy sauce

⅓ cup (2½ fl oz/80 ml) liquid smoke (optional)

½ cup (4 fl oz/125 ml) chicken stock, strong and strained of fat

1 tbl parsley, finely chopped

1 small red jalapeño, finely diced

1 medium white onion

1 tbl cayenne

1 tbl garlic salt

Mix all thoroughly, don't taste it, it will scare you and besides most of the heat will be too fresh.

5 lb/2 kg chicken wings, tips knocked off, but not
   cut in half.

1 cup (8 fl oz/250 ml) ketchup
1 tbl soy sauce

ALLOW 4 WINGS PER PERSON IF YOU ARE SERVING THEM AS AN APPETIZER

Drop the wings in the marinade, leave for 1 hour. Then bake at 350°F/180°C/gas mark 4 for 15 minutes in marinade. Remove, turn a few times, and let cool. Remove wings from sauce and place on a grill pan. Mix the ketchup and soy sauce with the main sauce and use to baste wings whilst cooking. Turn a few times, grilling time will only be a few minutes.

An alternative way to cook wings is to deep fry them from frozen. As soon as they stop 'talkin', they are cooked. Drain them, toss them in a mix of Durkee's (a thick hot sauce, to the uninitiated) and melted butter, then serve. Ghastly!

Maybe keep some cooked wings aside for a later salad - cut each wing in half and leave in the basting sauce in the fridge. Meanwhile, make a salad base with mango, roast bell peppers, lettuces and Italian dressing, toss, and serve the wings across the top.

Another easy chicken salad is batter-fried strips of chicken breast sitting on a lettuce base, dressed with Ranchhouse style dressing and tossed with pecans, cooked sweetcorn, and cooked black-eyed peas (cowpeas).

Chicken Bonne Femme

This dish is very traditional (I hope I don't have to say that again). Bonne femme is represented in the majority of cuisines. All it means is chicken sitting on a bed of rich gravy, with potatoes and bacon. It can look fancy and can also be cooked up quickly as good comfort food. In the original French version, the whole bird was roasted with the bacon and potatoes. I find it much easier to make the sauce in advance.

4 raw chicken breasts (supremes) with wing
   bone in

1 medium white onion, finely diced

1 medium green bell pepper

2 tbl (1 oz/25 g) butter

4 rashers streaky bacon, chopped and fried in
   finely chopped garlic

1 tbl Cajun seasoning (p. 19)

1 tbl dark roux (p. 21)

1 cup (8 fl oz/250 ml) chicken stock

1 cup (8 fl oz/250 ml) red wine

1 cup (8 oz/250 g) mushrooms, chopped

2 tbl olive oil

2 tbl soy sauce

2 cloves garlic, chopped

2 tbl parsley, finely chopped

1 portion frings (p. 95) or shoestring sweet
   potatoes, to serve

Serves 4

Sauté onion and bell pepper in the butter until soft. Add bacon and seasoning. Cook for five minutes. Add roux, as soon as the roux is melted add chicken stock and wine. Once it reaches simmering point, add mushrooms, and remove from heat. Sprinkle chicken with oil, soy, garlic, and parsley. Turn the heat up high and grill the chicken, turning twice.

Spread the sauce over the serving plates, top with a supreme, and smother the chicken with frings or shoestring sweet potatoes.

Chicken and Dumplings

Home cooking, deserves to be seen more in restaurants as it would show whether chefs in white hats can cook honestly. Just don't forget to sop up the gravy. Dumplings are real satisfying food.

Dumplings

2 cups (10 oz/250 g) plain flour
2¹/₂ tsp baking powder
¹/₄ tsp white pepper

1 tsp garlic salt
About 1 cup (8 fl oz/250 ml) milk

Chicken

1 3lb/1 kg chicken
2 cups (10 oz/250 g) chopped scallions (spring
   onions)

2 cups (10 oz/250 g) parsley, finely chopped
2 cups (10 oz/250 g) carrots, chopped

Gravy

2 cups (16 fl oz/500 ml) stock
1 cup (5 oz/125 g) diced mushrooms
1 tsp nutmeg

1 tsp cayenne
1 tsp garlic salt

SERVES 4-6

To make the dumplings, combine the flour, with the baking powder, white pepper, garlic salt, and with your fingers, mix gently together. Using as much milk as it takes (go by feel, there is no exact recipe), form the mixture into a dough and roll it out into 4-in/10cm strips.

Place the chicken in a large pot, add the scallions (spring onions), 2 cups of finely chopped parsley, 2 cups of chopped carrot. Cover with water and cook for one hour. Remove chicken, let cool, then remove the meat from the bone.

To make the gravy, add to the stock the diced mushrooms, nutmeg, cayenne, garlic salt and if desired to speed up the cooking add ¹/₂ cup of a light roux. Simmer for half an hour then add the chicken meat and drop in dumplings. Cover and cook for a further 20-30 minutes. Check seasoning and serve.

Garlic-Roasted Guinea Fowl with Dirty Rice and Cream Gravy

The guinea fowl, pintade in French, comes, not surprisingly, from West Africa. Many theories abound with regard to its history. To me the guinea fowl is one of the few commercially available birds to have any flavor. It looks like a cross between a chicken, a pheasant, and a turkey with a vulture's head. But less of that, they are fairly common these days and well worth the effort to track down and cook. So, consequently, do not chuck it in the microwave and nuke it.

Guinea fowl are sort of scrawny, so easy to overcook, but they do lend themselves to good portioning and quick cooking. If you don't fancy fixing guinea fowl, as they are so pretty, use them as guard dogs, much more effective than geese.

If it is just for two of you, it's easy to cut the bird in half and roast it. For a large dinner party, cutting up the bird actually stretches it further. Game birds differ from domesticated and broiler fowl. Guinea fowl have a good amount of meat on their backs. You may wish to carve it accordingly.

1 guinea fowl (about 2½ lb/1 kg), cut in half
4 tbl olive oil
1 tbl garlic salt

1 tbl garlic powder
1 large white onion, grated (reserve the juice)

Serves 2

In a large bowl, 'How large Chef?!', evenly cover the bird with the oil, then sprinkle with seasoning. Keep turning until covered. Combine with the onion, and keep tossing until bird is covered. Broil under a high heat, preferably a flame grill, basting with residual oil, seasoning, and juices. Make sure skin is in place. It is ready.

Dirty Rice

Dirty rice is a one-pot dish and can either be a main course or , as I prefer, a side-order. You cook the trinity and stock, and seasoning as usual. Add scraps and innards of your chicken(s) and some ground (minced) meats. Once boiling, add rice, and cook. Some folk add sausage. I feel it is unnecessary. Ensure you keep stirring and scraping the bottom of the pot. Lose the flame before the rice is actually cooked. Your rice will be dirty and tasting mighty fine. Dirty Rice is sometimes called the 'Louisiana Rice Dressing.'

2 pints/1.2 litres chicken stock

4 tbl oil

1 cup (5 oz/125 g) chicken livers, diced; add any scraps of chicken you may have

2 cups (10 oz/250 g) lean ground pork

1 tbl paprika

1 tsp garlic salt

1 tsp ground black pepper

1 tsp cayenne

1 tsp onion powder

3 cups (1 lb/450 g) long-grain white rice

2 chopped scallions (spring onions) for garnish

FOR THE TRINITY

1 cup (5 oz/125 g) red bell pepper, coarsely chopped

1 cup (5 oz/125 g) celery, coarsely chopped

1 cup (5 oz/125 g) onion, coarsely chopped

A very easy dish to prepare. Sauté trinity in the oil until the onion is soft, stir in chicken livers and pork, add seasoning as soon as pork is browned, and cook for further 10 minutes. Top with chicken stock, bring to simmer, and add rice. Keep stirring. Garnish with chopped scallions (spring onions).

Cream Gravy

1 cup (8 fl oz/250 ml) strong chicken stock

½ tsp garlic salt

½ tsp black pepper, coarse ground

1 small white onion, grated

½ cup (4 fl oz/125 ml) double cream

Bring the chicken stock to the boil. Add the garlic salt, black pepper and grated onion. Take off the heat as soon as the stock begins to boil again and mix in the double cream. Keep warm.

White Bean Chili

The key to this chili is the mild flavor of cumin. I find using up old cornbread or hush puppies works great with it.

4 tbl oil

2 cups (10 oz/250 g) cooked turkey meat

4 cups (1¾ pints/1 litre) chicken stock

1 tbl Cajun seasoning (see p. 19)

1 tsp cumin

1 tbl tomato purée

3 cups (1 lb/450 g) tomato, peeled, cored, and coarsely chopped

3 cups (1 lb/450 g) white haricot beans, cooked thoroughly

2 cups (10 oz/250 g) cooked chicken meat

1 cup (5 oz/125 g) crumbled corn bread

4 tbl sour cream

2 scallions (spring onions), finely chopped

FOR THE TRINITY

1 cup (5 oz/125 g) red bell pepper, coarsely chopped

1 cup (5 oz/125 g) celery, coarsely chopped

1 cup (5 oz/125 g) onion, coarsely chopped

SERVES 4-6

Sauté trinity with turkey until onion is soft. Bring stock to boil and add seasoning. Cook for 10 minutes then add tomato purée and chopped tomatoes. Add beans and chicken, turn off heat, add trinity mix. Stir well then add cornbread, leave covered. To serve, heat until the liquid has disappeared. Garnish with sour cream and scallions.

STEAK AND
OTHER GAMES

'First Catch Your 'Coon'

'Poor folk seek meat for their stomachs
rich folk stomachs for their meat.'

Not long ago, cooks in the UK and America were wary of using animal meats and ingredients which Escoffier or their mother had used quite freely. If you went back a little further you would have seen their relatively common appearance at the dinner table. Nowadays, chefs experiment with anything and everything from venison to beaver tails, to jicama to porcini mushrooms. I think I am all for it, especially when we can forget about joining the local gun club. Nowadays, your credit card and phone can usually bag you some game.

Venison is probably the most common game to be found. The word comes from the Latin 'venatus,' which simply means 'to hunt.' It is a rather loose term. In Britain, it refers mainly to the red deer. Over in the States, it covers any of the antlered game animals in the Cervidae family: elk, moose, whitetail, blacktail, mule deer, caribou, and various exotic farmed animals like antelope. Venison is leaner than beef, has no fat marbling to speak of, is lower in cholesterol, higher in protein, and generally free of chemical additives. It has an agreeable flavor, which is easily accepted.

As with venison and wild boar, quail and buffalo pose no problem either, I can live with eating game to that extent. But the menu at Jack's Firehouse in Philadelphia gets me. Jack McDavid, the chef, is a serious guy. He believes in the countryside and in the small farmer. Yet he cooks up a Beaver and Possum Hobo Stew, Sirloin of South Dakota Bear, and Snapping Turtle Soup.

Fricassée de Chevreuil aux Topinambours

(Venison and Artichoke Stew)

My marinade for venison is the essential element in this stew. It will need at least a few days chilling in the marinade, a new angle on hanging. The marinade consists of cider vinegar, garlic salt, coarsely ground black pepper, soy sauce, onion powder, and V-8 juice.

6 lb/2 ½ kg haunch of venison, cubed	2 cloves garlic, finely chopped
6 tbl (3 oz/75 g) butter	1 cup (5 oz/125 g) mushrooms, diced
1 large red bell pepper, diced	1 small red jalapeño
1 medium white onion, sliced	1 tsp garlic salt
1 cup (5 oz/125 g) smoked ham, diced	1 tsp white pepper
3 cups (1 lb/450 g) artichokes (I prefer canned)	1 bottle red wine

SERVES 6-8

Brown the venison in butter with the onion for 5 minutes. Add the bell pepper, onion, smoked ham, artichokes, garlic, and mushrooms. Mix in the jalapeño, garlic salt, and pepper. Add half the red wine. Cover with water and cook for 10 minutes, then add more red wine. Cover pot and cook over a low heat for 60-90 minutes. Serve over buttered noodles.

Hunter's Platter

Serve four different types of game with four different sauces around a centerpiece of creamed potatoes, or maybe go fancy and prepare Potatoes Teri – sliced potatoes covered in cream, grated cheese, and cilantro (coriander) with chopped tasso liberally mixed in, then baked until the top is crispy. I'll let you play with the various permutations on the game front, but if you have a special meal to prepare this is a winner. How about quail, venison, wild boar, and pheasant breasts?

Prepare four different stocks with the different games; you may need to label them! Make a strong reduction, then add each one to a Basic Hunter's Sauce. Don't lose the labels!

Basic Hunter's Sauce

1 large white onion, grated	1 tbl Worcestershire Sauce
2 tbl (1 oz/25 g) butter	1 cup (8 fl oz/250 ml) red wine
1 cup (8 fl oz/250 ml) mushroom ketchup	1 tsp cayenne
3 cups (1¼ pints/750 ml) chicken stock	1 tsp garlic salt
1 tbl soy sauce	4 tbl ketchup (preferably home-made)

Sauté the onion in butter first, add the mushroom ketchup, chicken stock, soy sauce, Worcestershire Sauce and red wine. Bring to boil, add cayenne, garlic salt, and ketchup. Reduce to a syrupy consistency by boiling over high heat for 15 minutes.

Squirrel Brunswick Stew

This stew either comes from Brunswick County in North Carolina or Brunswick County in Virginia. The basic meat was once squirrel, but it is now more frequently made with chicken or other meats. Thomas Jefferson hunted squirrel and loved this stew. Squirrel tastes a little like rabbit, but more delicate.

2-3 medium sized squirrels	3 rashers streaky bacon, diced and fried
Salt and pepper	2 medium white potatoes, diced
2 medium white onions, sliced	2 cups (10 oz/250 g) tomatoes, diced
1 cup (5 oz/125 g) cooked butter beans	1 tbl medium roux (p. 21)
1 cup (5 oz/125 g) sweetcorn	1 tsp sage

Prepare squirrels and cut into serving pieces. Season with salt and pepper. Boil the squirrel in water for 40 minutes. Add the corn and the beans; cook for 20 minutes. Add onion and bacon cook for 10 minutes. Check seasoning, add potatoes, tomatoes and roux; cook for 30 minutes. Taste. Take off the heat and leave in a warm place with the lid on for 20 minutes. Serve.

This is a meal in itself served with cornmeal muffins on the side.

My Brunswick stew is a simple version. You may wish to experiment by adding extra meats, such as chicken and rabbit. Ham bones will also prove a good addition. However, I don't feel the need for carrots and celery, as some folk do. They also prefer a funkier seasoning, but if your squirrels are fresh they should not need it. Remember not to eat red squirrels.

For more game recipes, buy Barbara Flood's recipe book 'Game in the Kitchen', published by Barre in 1969, it's wild. Here are some excerpts, although I stopped at listing 'woodcock entrail appetizers'.

'Cook the lungs of deer, moose, or wild boar in 4 tablespoons of vinegar per quart of salted water for 20 minutes.'

'Brer possum is grand eating, if you have an open mind and the fortitude to dispel thoughts of his somewhat unsavory appetite and his rat-like tree-swinging.'

'Young crows are.....generally fat and taste like pigeon.'

A must for all Nimrods I guess.

Ya Ca Mein

This is really the melting pot dish – Chinaman meets Cajun, and I'm not talking cricket. The Chinese arrived in Louisiana in the 1860s, when Lee Yuen of Canton moved there to exploit the burgeoning rice-growing. Instead, he became embroiled in the local shrimp industry and started a shrimp-drying business. After the shrimp dried in the sun, the Chinese fishermen and their families would dance on the shells – 'the Chinese Waltz' – to remove the shrimp.

The dried shrimp were then shipped all over the States and even back home to China. Because of the lack of refrigeration, the demand for Lee's shrimp was huge. However, this was a situation which did not last, leaving a legacy of only a few Chinese folk in the South. One is Sam, who owns the pool hall over in Desire, a neighborhood of New Orleans. Sam serves some awesome one-pot meals. Ya Ca Mein is a serious example.

This is a big recipe and it is probably best to plan well ahead – even cook it the day before. But it is definitely worth it. Read the recipe in full before starting. Try and buy the oxtails fresh and whole, they are best that way, and this allows you to decide the size of cut for the dish. The tails themselves are a bit of an education too, you'll see what I mean.

As mentioned, it may be easier to prepare the meats a day early. Thus, before dinner, all you have to do is begin the recipe from mushrooms onwards. More time for discussing the new Hawaiian shirt Barry just bought you, of course he had to get one made out of rayon.

SERVES 6-8

Meats

1 cup (5 oz/125 g) tasso or other smoked ham, diced	*About 4 tbl oil*
	2 oxtails, cut into sections
3 cups (1 lb/450 g) andouille sausage, sliced	*2 lb/1 kg beef short ribs*

146

Fry the tasso and sausage in a little oil to lose fat. Remove nad set aside the meats. Keep the residual oil in the pan.

Seasoning

1 tsp garlic salt	*1 tsp garlic powder*
2 tsp coarse-ground black pepper	*1 tsp oregano*
2 tsp paprika	*1 tsp thyme*
1 tsp cayenne	

Combine all in large bowl. Add the oxtails. Then brown in the reserved fat, it may take a little more oil. Remove the oxtails, add flour to pan and make a small roux.

Stock

About 3 cups (1¼ pints/750 ml) chicken stock	*5 small turnips, cut in half*
1 large white onion	*2 cups (10 oz/250 g) diced mushrooms*
3 leeks	*Salt and pepper*
3 stalks celery	*1½ cups (8 oz/200 g) beansprouts*
4 large carrots	*1 tbl Worcestershire Sauce*
1 medium red bell pepper	*Louisiana Hot Sauce*
2 cloves garlic, finely chopped	*To serve: 2 lb/1 kg cooked, buttered egg noodles*
4 tbl soy sauce	*6 scallions (spring onions), chopped*
1 cup (8 fl oz/250 ml) red wine	

Dice all the vegetables. Bring enough chicken stock to a simmer to cover veggies, add the roux and veggies, and cook for 10 minutes, stirring frequently. Add half the soy sauce and red wine. Cook five minutes then add all meats, including the ribs. Add the turnips. Cover the pot. Cook until oxtail and ribs are tender, stirring and scraping occasionally to stop meats sticking to the bottom of the pot. Cook for 2-3 hours. Have more chicken stock handy to keep the stew moist. Once the meats are tender, remove from the heat and add the diced mushrooms. Check seasoning. Keep warm and tightly covered until ready to serve.

Before serving, add the beansprouts and add the rest of the soy sauce, Worcestershire Sauce and hot sauce. Serve over buttered Chinese noodles and garnish with chopped scallions.

'Coon à la Delta

I cannot lie. I have never eaten a raccoon and I probably would not even be able to recognize the taste if described to me. They can taste of anything, acorns, your garbage, dead rabbits, anything! I have never even seen one alive. Same with possum but at least I know they will be greasy and stringy. I am told though, if you cannot find a raccoon down at the cornershop, you may substitute wild rabbit, I did.

Some folk like to just stuff their 'coon with sweet potatoes and then roast it. Others just roast. 'Coon à la Delta is a little more interesting. Maybe because we are all so squeamish, coupled with the fact that our countryside is bereft of wildlife, we limit ourselves to rabbit and venison. I fancy trying penguin. I believe we could have a whole load of fun cooking up weird animals which thrive around and about. I note that the Italians of Sienna, at Palio, cook around 3,000 song thrushes at each festival.

Skin and clean your raccoon, then refrigerate for at least 24 hours. A medium-sized 'coon will serve four.

1 young 'coon, cut into serving pieces
2 cups (8 oz/250 g) seasoned flour for dusting
  'coon
½ cup (5 oz/125 g) butter
1 tsp Worcestershire Sauce
1 tbl Louisiana Hot Sauce

Salt and pepper to taste
3 cloves garlic, finely chopped
1 cup trinity (equal quantities of finely chopped
  bell pepper, onion, and celery)
6 medium sweet potatoes, each cut in half

Roll the 'coon in flour. Brown the 'coon in butter then add water to cover, Worcestershire Sauce, hot sauce, and seasoning to taste. Cook 10 minutes then remove the 'coon. Add the garlic and trinity to the saucepan and simmer for 20 minutes, reduce them to gravy.

Place 'coon in a roasting tray, surround with sweet potatoes. Baste with gravy. Bake at 350°F/180°C/ gas mark 4 until sweet potatoes are fork-tender. The 'coon will be ready too. Serve with butter beans and macquechoux (see p. 124). Enjoy.

If you hunt for your own 'coon, then you will know it's thirsty work. Maybe next time you should prepare a pitcher of Lynchburg Coonhunter's Punch. To make the punch, marinate lemon and pineapple overnight in brandy. Late next morning add rum, tea, sugar, and Bourbon. That night, when you return from hunting serve the mix over ice, in chilled glasses. Top with champagne. Doesn't matter if you failed to catch any 'coons.

Tasso

There is a little saying in South Louisiana which runs along the lines of 'the only part of the pig the Cajuns don't eat is the squeal.' Well, they are poor folk. Tasso (tah-so) is proof the Cajuns do not want to waste what God has kindly sent their way. It is heavily seasoned scraps of pork which are unsuitable for any other use. It is then smoked. It is mainly used as a flavoring agent, adding zest and spice to many dishes. Today, Tasso is produced commercially and is sometimes quite edible.

Bruce Aidells, a fine Californian chef, makes it by rubbing brine-cured pickled pork with a blend of herbs and spices. He then air-dries it and finally cold-smokes it. If you are lucky enough to come across some in a store, use it sparingly as it will be very hot. It is best, in my opinion, to make your own substitute.

1 tbl paprika
1 tbl garlic salt
1 tbl cayenne
1 tbl coarse-ground black pepper
1 tbl hot sauce
½ tbl thyme

½ tbl onion powder
½ tbl cinnamon
3 lb/1½ kg shoulder ham, thinly sliced
1 medium white onion, grated
2 tbl oil

Mix all seasonings. Drop in ham and coat, then refrigerate. We should smoke it at this point, but don't worry if you can't.

Sauté onion in oil and hot sauce, it's best to do this separately, so you don't knock the seasoning off the ham. Transfer the ham to a baking tray and pour the seasoned oil over it. It will now be heavily seasoned. Bake at 325°F/170°C/gas mark 3 for 90 minutes to 2 hours. Turn once or twice. Allow to cool before touching, although the ham may need loosening from the tray.

I have no idea where the name 'tasso' comes from.

Andouille Sausage

Once you have made your own sausages, a labor of love gone into their preparation, and the flavors extracted from the fresh herbs and special meats, it will spoil you for ever. The thought of plastic-wrapped store-bought products will begin to nauseate you. But if you must go to the store go to Mrs Lyon, Jacob Andouille, La Place, Louisiana. Her sausages are good.

Andouille is a spicy smoked sausage and ubiquitous in Louisiana cooking. Don't even consider substituting the French version (andouillette), which is completely different. Louisiana andouille is simply made from lean pork and buckets of seasoning, including mace, and it is cold-smoked. Here's a few other Southern favorites:

Chaurice

Chaurice or hot sausage is an adaptation of the Spanish chorizo, a legacy from the Spanish. It is much spicier than any other sausage in the South and thus not too common in cooking. Again it is a pork sausage, but it is sold fresh, i.e., not smoked.

Chorizo

Chorizo is a generic name for sausage, thus it covers various products throughout the Spanish-speaking world. Fortunately in the UK it appears to have a sole guise, so I can refer to it with confidence. Chorizos are not as spicy as my favorite andouille, but have a variety of flavors produced by the spices cumin and coriander. Ensure you source a supplier with a distinctive and consistent supply, not a supermarket.

Boudin

'The smell is the first thing you notice…Most people can't wait to get home or even into the car. Standing in the hot sun with your Dixie beer or Barq's root beer in your left hand, you get one end of the hot boudin in your right hand and put the other in your mouth…and squeeze…Hot Boudin!'

Each area of Louisiana has its own way of making this sausage which has been a favorite for 200 years or so, and is an integral part of charcuterie. Driving around southern Louisiana you will come across bumper stickers reading 'BEWARE! DRIVER EATING BOUDIN.' Boudin are meant to be spicy. The primary ingredients are pork, pork liver, onion, green (spring) onion, parsley, cayenne, black pepper, salt and rice. It is like a moist dressing in a casing. I prefer them steamed to order, but grilling and baking work fine. I had great success with a crawfish boudin I made for Mardi Gras.

Pickled Watermelon Rind

The side-roads in the South seem to be lined with small stalls and stores selling a mess of wonderful, homegrown produce. In the late spring, most of them begin selling watermelons. Like coconuts, watermelons are an effort to eat, but they are much more refreshing and fun. The rinds also make this fine preserve, and not just for breakfast.

6-7 cups (2 lb/900 g) watermelon rinds, green
  skin and red flesh removed, chopped into
  cubes
1/3 cup (2 1/2 oz/100 g) sea salt
About 4 pints/2.5 litres water
2 tsp salt

2 cups (16 fl oz/500 ml) cider vinegar
1 1/2 cups (12 1/2 oz/375 g) sugar
1 tsp allspice
1 tsp whole cloves
1 tsp cinnamon
1 tsp ginger

Soak the watermelon rinds in sea salt and water to cover overnight. Drain, add 4 cups (1 3/4 pints/1 litre) of water and salt, boil until tender. Boil vinegar with sugar and spices for 15 minutes. Add rinds and boil gently for 5-10 minutes. Cool. Pour into preserving jars and seal.

Jalapeño Jelly

'C'est piquant le Diable avec le douceur d'un ange.'

This will kill you, skinny legs and all. Jalapeños have a wonderful taste and give off vibrant flavors. Maybe serve with pickled pigs' feet or use as a condiment with steaks or maybe even as a Christmas present – Gran'ma will love you even more. Pectin is a setting agent, naturally found in certain fruits.

1 red bell pepper, finely diced
6 green jalapeños, skinned, de-veined and finely
  diced
1 cup (8 fl oz/250 ml) cider vinegar
4 cups (1 1/4 lb/500 g) white sugar

1 tbl parsley, very finely chopped
3 scallions (spring onions), diced
2 tbl lemon juice
1 6 fl oz/175 ml bottle of pectin

Boil all the ingredients except the lemon juice and pectin for 15 minutes. Remove from the heat and add lemon and pectin. Stir very well. Pour into preserving jars and seal. Chill. Give a good stir before transferring to a serving bowl.

Buttermilk Bisquits

One of many fine Southern specialties rarely attempted by myself are these buttermilk bisquits. I have learned how to bake them (though I still prefer Pillsbury's version – POP!) My success encouraged me to explore. Sweet Potato Bisquits are wild and after mastering them I just had to make Banana Bread. But isn't it funny how breads these days are so fashionable? I guess some folks' moms never baked.

2 cups (10 oz/250 g) strong, plain flour
1 tbl baking powder
3 tbl sugar
2 tsp salt

1 cup (8 fl oz/250 ml) buttermilk
5 tbl (2½ oz/60 g) white cooking fat or lard
About ½ cup (5 oz/125 g) melted butter for brushing

Pre-heat oven to 450°F/230°C/gas mark 8. Sift the dry ingredients, mix the buttermilk and fat, fold the liquid into the dry ingredients. Beat thoroughly until you have a smooth dough. Roll out the dough until it is ¼ in/5 mm thick. Cut into 2½ in/5 cm rounds. Brush with butter. Bake for ten minutes. Enjoy.

Maybe just eat the bisquits all by yourself, smothered with pork or beef debris.

Sweet Potato Bisquits

5 cups (1½ lb/750 g) boiled sweet potatoes
1 tsp vanilla essence
2 cups (10 oz/250 g) strong, plain flour
1 tsp baking powder
½ tsp cinnamon

½ tsp allspice
½ tsp salt
½ cup (2½ oz/60 g) brown sugar
3 tbl (1½ oz/40 g) softened butter
4 eggs

Mash the potatoes with the vanilla essence. Sift the flour, spices, salt and sugar together. Beat the butter and eggs. Beat the liquid into the dry ingredients. Beat thoroughly until you have a smooth dough. Roll out the dough until it is ¼ in/5 mm thick. Shape it as required. Bake in a pre-heated 375°F/190°C/gas mark 5 oven until for 25 minutes or until lightly browned.

Banana Bread

4 medium overripe bananas (they should be
    black)
1 cup (5 oz/125 g) brown sugar
2 eggs, beaten
1 cup (10 oz/250 g) unsalted butter, melted

2 cups (10 oz/250 g) plain flour
2 tsp baking powder
1/2 tsp cinnamon
1/2 tsp lemon juice
3 tbl buttermilk

Mash the bananas with the brown sugar and add eggs and butter - mix. Combine flour, baking powder, and cinnamon, then add to banana mix. Slowly add in buttermilk.

   Grease a loaf tin and transfer batter into it. Pre-heat oven to 350°F/180°C/gas mark 4. Bake bread for 30 minutes, lower heat to 300°F/150°C/gas mark 2. Bake for a further 30 minutes. Turn off oven and leave for 15-20 minutes. Check to ensure loaf is cooked through, by piercing with a skewer in the center. The loaf should be dark brown and the skewer should come out clean. Transfer to cooling rack. Serve as soon as it is cool.

Natchitoches Meat Pies

To my 'provincial' surprise meat pies are big news in certain parts of the South. Remember the movie 'Steel Magnolias'? Fabulous, a real weepy. The movie was set in Natchitoches (NACK-i-tish), on the north shore of Lake Pontchartrain. Prior to the movie, the town was only known for its baked meat pies. This, despite the fact that it is the oldest settlement in The Louisiana Purchase, founded in 1714.

   Serve Natchitoches Meat Pies with a spicy brown gravy, perhaps roast pecan gravy (see p. 178), and fresh yeasty rolls or, like the locals, eat them with a generous portion of dirty rice, as you would find at Lasyones Meat Pie Kitchen and Restaurant – the true home of this, Louisiana's answer to the empanada. Or maybe try, my preference for a side-dish, Hoppin' John (see below).

1 tbl oil for sautéing
1 medium onion, finely chopped
3 cups (1 lb/450 g) ground pork
3 cups (1 lb/450 g) ground beef
1 bunch scallions (spring onions), chopped
1 clove garlic, finely chopped
1 medium red bell pepper, diced small

1 tsp garlic salt
1 tsp cayenne pepper
1 tsp onion pepper
1 tbl soy sauce
1 tsp Worcestershire Sauce
1 lb/450 g shortcrust pastry, chilled

Now most folk have made a flavored mince dish, right? This is the aim here. Brown the meats with the onion, add all the other ingredients and cook fast for a short period. Cool. Roll out the dough and cut out rounds, saucer size. Spoon a small amount of the meat mixture into the middle of each round. Fold over into half-moon shapes. Fry to order in the oil. Easy. This recipe makes around 18 pies, but they will go quick. Trust me.

Hoppin' John

Black-eyed peas (also known in the UK as black-eyed beans) are a very popular ingredient in the Southern States and the basis for this wonderfully named dish. In South Carolina, they have a vegetarian dish of okra and rice, which is very similar and is called 'Limpin' Susan'. Traditionally, Hoppin' John is served on New Year's Eve, to ensure good luck and prosperity for the coming year. The first mention of the dish was in 1838. However, where the name originates is anyone's guess. I like John Thorne's idea that it came from the corruption of 'pois à pigeon' – say it fast. Pigeon peas were, and probably still are, popular in the Caribbean and the name traveled with the émigrés.

12 oz /300 g black-eyed peas
1 small white onion, finely chopped
1 small green bell pepper, finely chopped
1 stick celery, finely chopped
1 small red bell pepper, finely chopped
2 pints/1.2 litres chicken stock
5 rashers streaky bacon, chopped small

4 oz/100 g tasso or salted ham
1 tsp paprika
1 tsp garlic salt
1 tsp cayenne
1 tsp white pepper
1 cup (5 oz/125 g) long-grain rice
3 chopped scallions (spring onions)

Soak the peas in cold water overnight, then boil in fresh water for 15 minutes. Discard water. Bring the peas to boil in 2 pints/1.2 litres stock. Meanwhile, sauté the vegetables, bacon and ham. Remove from heat and mix in seasonings.

Cook the rice separately and keep warm. (It can be cooked together, but you would lose definition and texture). As soon as the peas are soft, mix in veggies and rice. Mix thoroughly. Drain off excess liquid if necessary and mix in scallions. Serve.

Limpin' Susan

2 lb/1 kg okra
5 tbl (2½ oz/50 g) butter
2 small red jalapeños, finely diced
1 tsp white pepper
1 tsp cayenne
1 tsp paprika
1 tsp celery salt
1 tsp onion powder

1 cup (5 oz/125 g) cooked long grain rice

FOR THE TRINITY

1 cup (5 oz/125 g) green bell pepper, finely
   chopped
1 cup (5 oz/125 g) celery, finely chopped
1 cup (5 oz/125 g) white onion, grated

Slice the okra into 5 or 6 pieces per pod, including tops. Sauté okra in butter for 5 minutes. Remove it and add the trinity, cook for 5 minutes. Add jalapeños. Mix okra into warm rice, add trinity and seasoning. Keep in oven for 15 minutes before serving. Stir well and eat.

Stewed Okra

I already feel you wanting to skip this recipe. DON'T ! Okra, in the right hands, is delightful. Be it in a gumbo or plain cornmeal-fried, you can even use it in the wet Hush Puppy mix. Trust me, you will start to appreciate my buddy Hibiscus esculentus.

1 cup (5 oz/125 g) okra	*1 tsp cayenne*
1 onion, sliced	*1 tsp dried thyme*
1 green bell pepper, de-seeded, de-veined and	*½ cup (2½ oz/60 g) andouille*
* sliced*	*½ cup (2½ oz/60 g) smoked ham*
4 tbl oil	*1 cup (5 oz/125 g) tomatoes, skinned and diced*
1 tsp sea salt	

Sauté the onion and green bell pepper in the oil. Add the seasonings. Drop in the sliced smoked sausage and diced ham, keep stirring. After 5 minutes remove from heat. Add the tomatoes, mix in. Transfer to a casserole or heavy-based saucepan. Cut the okra crosswise and mix into pan. Bake for 15 minutes in a pre-heated oven at 350°F/180°C/gas mark 4 with lid on. Remove from oven, don't look in, and then serve at table.

Andouille and Potatoes

Perfect for a snack or as a side-dish, although I have presented it here as a main course lunch dish. Try serving with Past Caring Onion Rings (p. 158) or with a poached egg riding high.

4 medium potatoes , thinly sliced

½ cup (2½ oz/60 g) green bell pepper, diced

1 cup (5 oz/125g) grated onion

4 tbl oil

1½ andouille sausages, sliced thin

3 rashers streaky bacon, diced

1 tsp cayenne

1 tsp garlic salt

1 cup (8 fl oz/250 ml) white wine

1 tbl soy sauce

2 cups (10 oz/250 g) mushrooms

2 scallions (spring onion), chopped

Sauté potatoes, pepper and onion until the edges of the potato brown. You will need to keep stirring. Add sausage, bacon, and seasoning, using the wine to loosen. Cook for a further 5 minutes, then add soy sauce and mushrooms. Serve immediately. Garnish with chopped scallions.

As a variation, I have drained the mix, removed a few potatoes, and served over chopped spinach for a brunch-style salad. I actually topped it with poached quails' eggs.

Past Caring Onion Rings

These have to be thick and wide. Ensure you coat them twice in batter, then chill on trays for around one hour. This way, the batter absorbs onion flavor. If you can only find small onions, forget it, maybe use bell pepper rings instead.

Use a buttermilk batter, maybe add Parmesan cheese to it.

Cabbage and Ham Hock

You can use leftover hocks from the soups, but you will have a mighty satisfying dish if you start from scratch. This way you retain all the stock from the ham, in which you can braise the cabbage. Very warming on a cold day or after a tough day's fishing.

1 small to medium ham hock
Water to cover
1 white onion, sliced
2 garlic cloves, crushed

1 tsp garlic salt
1 tsp cayenne
1 medium white cabbage

SERVES 4-6

In a large pot, simmer the hock in water for a about three hours. Add more water, sliced white onion, and flattened garlic cloves. Pull out the hock, let cool and pull the meat off and coarsely chop, return the meat and bone to the pot. Add a little garlic salt and cayenne. Keep cooking. Core and chop the cabbage. Add to pot and cook for a further 45 minutes or until the stock has reduced to a gravy. Serve with fresh bread rolls.

Hogshead Cheese

(headless version)

If you have a big enough pot, this is a great dish to attempt. Of course it is not for the squeamish and you may have a few problems buying the main ingredient at the local supermarket. I once cooked up three heads in the same stock pot and, what I thought was a bit of fun, ended up with a waitress in tears and being begged to retract her resignation.

Hogshead cheese, 'fromage de tête de porc', is a terrine. Some make it into a sausage, made out of a calf's head or a pig's head. It molds into

159

shape due to the jelly found in the head and requires little seasoning, in my opinion; others disagree. In the U.K., it is called 'brawn.'

2-3 pork knuckles	1 medium white onion, diced
3 pig's trotters	1 cup (5 oz/125 g) celery, diced
1 calf's tongue (optional)	1 medium red onion, grated
8 pints/4.8 litres water	3 rashers streaky bacon
5 bay leaves	1 tbl white wine vinegar
1 tsp thyme	1 tsp crushed dried chiles
1 tsp nutmeg	1 tbl parsley, finely chopped
1 clove garlic, finely chopped	5 tbl (2½ oz/60 g) butter
1 cup (5 oz/125 g) carrot, diced	

SERVES 4-6

Place the meats in a large pot of water and bring to boil. Add first bay leaf, thyme, nutmeg, and garlic then carrot, white onion, and celery. Simmer for 4-5 hours. Meanwhile, sauté red onion with bacon, vinegar, chile, and parsley in the butter until bacon is slightly crisp. Remove pork from pot, scrape off meat and discard bones.

Boil up liquid until thick. Take off heat and add the fried bacon mix. Pour the liquid over the pork and stir. Fill a lightly-buttered terrine dish, or whatever suitable dish you have. Chill overnight.

To loosen the cheese from the pan, quickly drop the base in hot water. Invert and slice. Serve at room temperature. If you serve when the head cheese is chilled some of the flavors will be dormant.

Daube Glacé or New Orleans Daube of Beef

Similar to Hogshead cheese, but an old French style of cooking. It is a piece of beef braised with veal and pig's feet and allowed to cool in it's own jelly. It resembles a fancy pâté, but tastes infinitely better. It is a tradition to serve Daube Glacé at Cajun weddings.

1 ham hock
4-6 pig's trotters
4 garlic cloves, crushed
1 cup (5 oz/125 g) parsley, finely chopped
4 tbl Cajun seasoning (p. 19)
2 pints/1.2 litre chicken stock
4 lb/2 kg joint of beef
3 lb/1.5 kg pork butt or veal shoulder
4 tbl garlic salt

4 tbl coarse-ground black pepper
2 tbl oil

FOR THE TRINITY

3 cups (1 lb/450 g) green bell pepper, coarsely chopped
3 cups (1 lb/450 g) celery, coarsely chopped
3 cups (1 lb/450 g) white onion, coarsely chopped

SERVES UP TO 12 FOLK

Boil the ham and pig's trotters with garlic, parsley, and seasoning in the chicken stock until the meat falls off.

Finely chop the trinity. Heat oven to 400°F/200°C/gas mark 6. Place the roasting meats on an oiled baking tray and quickly brown each side in the oven. Take out, sprinkle each side with garlic salt and black pepper. Place trinity and little oil and water in the pan and replace roasts. Reduce heat to 350°C/180°C/gas mark 4. Cook for 2-3 hours.

Remove from oven, coarsely chop meats, and mix in trinity. Then pour pork and stock over roasts. Press firm into dish. This is your daube, now refrigerate overnight or longer. I think it is best to serve Daube, unmolded, on top of warm greens. Enjoy.

Seared Calf's Liver with Spinach, Bacon and Red Wine Gravy

For a weekend special, I once ordered a calf's liver. The following morning, having been to the fish market, I was a little late arriving in for prep. My main guy had used his initiative and started everything off. One particular item he had started was the 'dirty rice' (chicken livers, ground pork, and rice). Being a Friday he had decided to produce a larger-than-normal batch. This one just happened to be that much larger.

I proceeded to prepare the specials, and despite the delivery note, could find no calf's liver. Following a little questioning the truth emerged. I queried Richard on the size of chickens in his native Ghana. It was an expensive, but excellent, dirty rice!

Anyway this dish is a winner, although a little pricey. In Britain, we traditionally serve bacon and onion with liver dishes. Here I add them both to the greens, which sit under the liver. I then drizzle a red wine gravy over the whole dish. This allows for a neat presentation and lets the delicate liver speak alone, at first anyway.

1 ¹/₂ lb/750 g liver (6 oz/175 g per person) calf's liver
6 tbl (3 oz/75 g) butter
1 medium red onion, grated
¹/₂ cup (2¹/₂ oz/60 g) tasso, diced small
1 tbl parsley, finely chopped
4 tbl brandy

1 white onion, sliced
2 rashers bacon, chopped
1 tsp garlic salt
1 tsp coarse-ground black pepper
¹/₂ cup (4 fl oz/125 ml) red wine
2 cups (10 oz/250 g) spinach
2 red jalapeños, chopped

Slice the liver into pieces 1 in/2.5 cm thick. Melt 2¹/₂ oz/60 g butter and sauté the onion, tasso, and parsley. As the tasso begins to brown add liver and brandy, increase the heat, and be attentive. Cook each side for 1-2 minutes each, depending on how you like your meat cooked. Just before serving, add more brandy. Serve on top of greens. Pour the tasso gravy into the greens.

Sauté sliced white onion in the rest of the butter and the bacon for 5 minutes. Add garlic salt and coarsely ground black pepper, loosen with wine and fold in chopped spinach. Take off heat and let finish. Sprinkle with finely chopped red jalapeños before arranging on plates.

Chicken-Fried Steak with Rice and Milk Gravy

Chicken-fried steak is another Southern staple. It is simply steak prepared in the same was as Southern fried chicken. It is more economical than grilled steak, as you can use cheaper cuts.

1¹/₂ lb/750 g steak (6 oz/175g per person)
2 eggs, beaten
1 cup (8 fl oz/250 ml) milk
2 cups (10 oz/250 g) flour seasoned with salt
  and pepper

Milk Gravy (p. 178)
3 cups (1 lb/450 g) cooked long-grain white rice,
  to serve

Slice the steak thinly and flatten with a steak hammer. You want them as big as your Dad's hand and about ¹/₂ inch/1 cm thick. Then prepare as for fried chicken. Dip in a egg-and-milk batter, dredge in seasoned flour and shallow fry for 10-15 minutes. Smother with Milk Gravy (p. 178), and serve rice on the side.

If you fancy being real special make Red Eye Gravy instead. This is a Southern gravy made from ham drippings and sometimes flavored with coffee. Prepare it and you will soon work out how it got its name.

Ribeye Steak with Garlic-Tasso-Mushroom Gravy

Cooking steaks is really up to you. I like them medium-rare, so I have the grill up real high and give each side 2-3 minutes. If I have room to baste, I will use soy sauce and Louisiana Hot Sauce. But the thing with steaks is the fun you can have with the side-orders. Why not try this gravy and the following fries. All you will need then is a big Cabernet-Sauvignon.

Or alternatively just grill the steaks, serve topped with Chardonnay-Shallot Butter and fresh yeasty rolls.

Chardonnay-Shallot Butter

1 cup (8 fl oz/250 ml) Chardonnay
4 small shallots, finely chopped

½ cup (4 oz/125 g) unsalted butter
½ tsp black pepper, freshly ground

Boil the wine with the shallots until reduced to a syrup. Mix them into the softened butter. Top with black pepper. Chill.

Garlic-Tasso-Mushroom Gravy

8 cloves garlic, finely chopped
1 medium red onion, diced
5 tbl (2½ oz/60 g) unsalted butter
1 tsp garlic salt
½ cup (4 fl oz/125 ml) red wine
1 tbl roux, peanut color (see p. 21)

1 cup (8 fl oz/250 ml) chicken stock
1 tsp ground white pepper
1 tsp coarse-ground black pepper
1 cup (5 oz/125 g) mushrooms, diced
½ cup (2½ oz/75 g) tasso, diced
½ cup (4 fl oz/125 ml) double cream

Sauté garlic and onion in butter for three minutes, add garlic salt and red wine, cook for 5 minutes. Warm together roux and chicken stock, add rest of seasoning. Add mushrooms and bring to boil for five minutes. Mix sauces together and keep warm.

When ready to serve, heat to nearly boiling point, add tasso and cream. Take off heat and keep stirring.

Buttermilk Chicken-Fried French Fries or Pickles

Make these hot and spicy and you will soon be asked when the next party is.

1 cup (8 fl oz/250 ml) buttermilk
1 cup (5 oz/125 g) plain flour
1 tsp garlic salt

1 tsp ground white pepper
1 tsp cayenne
1 lb/450 g frozen crinkle-cut chips

Make a batter with these ingredients. Pull crinkle cut fries from the freezer, drop in batter and deep fry. (My buddy from Miami even 'chicken- fries' chips - crisps - by dipping them in the batter then in flour).

But if I had to choose a potato to serve with a steak, it would be Soufflé Potatoes. These are bizarre potato chips which are deep-fried at two different temperatures, having spent 30 minutes in cold water in between the frying, to allow the fryer's temperature to rise. The second, hotter, frying causes the potatoes to puff up. Bizarre.

There is another little story behind them, but I imagine you are becoming bored of my anecdotal style by now. Right? So instead of soufflé potatoes I will give you a recipe for Brabant.

Brabant (brah-Bawhn) Potatoes

A popular New Orleans style of peppery potato, garlicky and crispy. A real 'stealing' snack.

6 waxy potatoes, diced roughly into bite-size
   pieces
1 cup (8 fl oz/250 ml) oil
1 medium white onion, grated

3 cloves garlic, finely chopped
1 tbl parsley, finely chopped
6 tbl (3 oz/75 g) butter
2 tsp garlic salt

Two points here, first, make too much, they are definitely 'moreish' and two, the double action of deep-frying and baking is important.

Keep the potatoes in water until you are ready to use them. Dry off the potatoes on kitchen towels and deep fry at 350°F/180°C for 3 minutes until soft. Shake off oil. Sauté onion, garlic, and parsley together in butter for 3 minutes. Add potatoes and coat well with the garlic salt. Transfer to baking dish and bake in a preheated 400°F/200°C/gas mark 6 oven for 15-20 minutes.

Smothered Pork Chops with Creamed Spinach

In the States, spinach undergoes many culinary attacks, in an attempt to disguise its flavor, texture, and even existence. Creamed, however, with subtle nutmeg flavoring, it is actually very tasty, providing none of the cooking liquid is lost.

3 tbl oil
4 pork chops
1 medium onion, sliced
2 sticks celery, diced
1 medium red bell pepper, diced

5 medium tomatoes
2 cups (16 fl oz/500 ml) chicken stock
1 cup (8 fl oz/250 ml) red wine
1 tbl Cajun seasoning (p. 19)

SERVES 4 (OR 6 IF YOU TAKE THE MEAT OFF THE BONE)

Sauté vegetables in oil for 5 minutes, add seasoning. Cook for 2 minutes and then brown chops. Lower heat, cover with tomatoes, stock, and wine. Cover with a tight-fitting lid and cook for 1 hour. Turn once or twice.

The drippings in any pan should never be discarded, particularly the debris from cooking pork. Mix in a little water, mix in all the debris, and double the quantity of liquid with coffee, cider, beer, or wine. Then reduce again.

Creamed Spinach

1 14 oz/400 g packet frozen spinach
1 medium onion, grated
1/2 cup (4 fl oz/125 ml) double cream
1 tsp nutmeg

1 tsp garlic salt
1/2 tsp celery salt
1 tsp ground white pepper
4 tbl grated Parmesan cheese

Cook onion with spinach until defrosted. Add the rest of ingredients and serve after 5 minutes. Garnish with grated Parmesan cheese.

Boston Butt Roast

The Boston butt is the top of the shoulder. You need to ask for two-thirds lean meat and one-third fat. Covering the roast with milk may seem a little excessive and a little strange. It will please you however. Serve the butt roast with creamed potatoes and gravy, perhaps the pan gravy or the ham-cream gravy. Black-olive mashed potatoes are fun.

5-6 lb/2-3 kg butt roast
8 cloves garlic, 6 finely chopped
About 2 pints/1.2 litres milk
1 large white onion, finely diced
1 medium red bell pepper, finely diced
About 1/2 cup (4 fl oz/125 ml) oil

1 tbl 3-way pepper seasoning (equal quantities, of cayenne, black pepper, and paprika)
1 cup (8 fl oz/250 ml) red wine
1 tbl dark roux (p. 21)
6 scallions (spring onions), chopped
2 tsp garlic salt

SERVES 6-8

Trim fat off outside of pork. Score the meat and rub with 2 fresh garlic cloves. Place in high-sided dish and cover with milk. Refrigerate over night. Keep the milk for gravy, or discard it.

Pre-heat oven to 250°F/130°C/gas mark ½. Place roast in baking tray, cover bottom of pan with 1 in/2.5 cm water and add onion and pepper. Sprinkle the top of roast with oil and sprinkle with 3-way seasoning. Cook for 5 hours. Remove roast, add wine, roux, scallions to pan, scrap in debris and mix until you have a thick gravy. Check seasoning and add garlic salt. Slice the roast and return to pan until ready for serving.

Ham-Cream Gravy

You can make a fresh ham-cream gravy with onions, white wine, and cream.

But you will get a real good flavor by using only half the roux you would usually use for a gravy base and mixing in a little butter and cream once the liquid has cooled a little.

Creamed Horseradish Potatoes

Another invention out of nowhere in particular, which became very popular. I don't think playing around with mashed potatoes is anything new. Try it yourself. Other examples I tried were the addition of bacon, cheese, hard-boiled eggs, crab, funky vegetables, diced shrimp, and once, smoked eel. (Be careful to buy your eel ready-smoked. I thought I'd be cute and smoke them myself, which means cooking them first. Trust me, they don't like hot water. They may also scare your girlfriend.) One success on the deviant mashed pots. scene was using chopped black olives.

3 cups (1 lb/450 g) white potatoes, mashed (use a hand masher for better texture)
1 medium white onion, grated
½ cup (4 fl oz/125 ml) milk
½ cup (4 fl oz/125 ml) double cream
1 tbl creamed horseradish

½ cup (2½ oz/60 g) parsley, finely chopped
1 tsp garlic salt
1 tsp ground white pepper
1 tsp coarse-ground black pepper
6 tbl (3 oz/75 g) unsalted butter
3 scallions (spring onions), chopped

With the potatoes still hot, combine all the ingredients except the butter. Melt 1 tablespoon of the butter and beat it in with the rest, then dot the mixture with the remaining butter. Place in a warm oven (325°F/170°C/gas mark 3) for at least 10 minutes or until needed. Garnish with chopped scallions.

Beef Boudreaux

Execute this right and your beau will think you are a real groovy cat, trust me. My recipe is a slight steal from Lamb Boudreaux by the Louisiana chef Alex Patout. Beef Boudreaux is sublime, probably the finest non-fish entrée I ever prepared.

If you cannot find crawfish, substitute diced shrimp. Be careful not to cut the beef too thin or overcook it. If you or your guests like well-done meat (what is wrong with you?) use a cheaper cut, or even lamb, as Mr Patout initially used.

1 lb/450 g beef fillet
1/2 cup (2 1/2 oz/60 g) tasso, diced small
4 scallions (spring onions), diced
1 small red bell pepper, diced small
1 cup (5 oz/125 g) tomatoes, cored and diced
1/2 cup (4 fl oz/125 ml) white wine
1 tsp garlic salt
1 tsp onion powder
1 tsp fresh thyme
1 tsp oregano

1 tbl 3-way pepper seasoning (equal quantities,
 of cayenne, black pepper, and paprika)
1/2 tbl tomato purée
1/2 cup (4 fl oz/125 ml) double cream
1 cup crawfish tails
Dash soy sauce (optional)
Dash Louisiana Hot Sauce (optional)
Chopped scallions (spring onions)
Parsley, finely chopped for garnish

SERVES 4-6

Cut the beef into 4 small medallions, about 5 ins/8 cm across and 1 in/2.5 cm thick. Make the sauce first, then cut and immediately grill the beef.

To make the sauce, sauté tasso and scallions in the butter and add bell pepper. After a few minutes, add tomatoes and wine. Bring to a simmer and add seasonings and tomato purée. Cook for a further 4-5 minutes, and add cream and crawfish. Stir and remove from heat. Place lid on and keep warm.

Grill beef under/over high heat, maybe sprinkle with soy and Hot Sauce. Meanwhile, sauté the potato cakes (see below). Re-heat sauce, assemble two beef slices over potato cakes pour the sauce over it. Seriously enjoy.

If you still fancy the Boudreaux sauce but, for whatever reason not the beef, use lamb medallions instead, or even use the sauce to top pasta.

Potato Cakes

These are fun as a starter, the base for a main course such as Beef Boudreaux, a side-order, or even as a breakfast item. You can make them up from scratch or just when you have left-over potatoes, whichever way, they are good.

3 cups (1 ½ lb/750g)mashed potatoes
1 medium white onion, grated
½ cup (2 oz/50 g) parsley, finely chopped
2 eggs beaten

1 tbl plain flour
1 tsp garlic salt
1 tsp coarse-ground black pepper
6 tbl (3 oz/75 g) butter

Combine the mashed potatoes with all the other ingredients except the butter. Make thin patties and fry until golden in the butter.

I enjoy making these, adding chopped shrimp, fish, or even cooked, shredded chicken, they are a fun versatile item. As a starter they are good with a rich, cream gravy garnished with snipped chives.

Bronzed Lamb Noisettes with Marchand de Vin

Lamb is king of the readily available red meats, in my book anyway. I rarely had it on the menus but, regularly brought it in for Iggy and his Albanian boys in the kitchen, because it reminded them of home.

Inform your guests what a 'noisette' is (the eye of the loin, completely boned) and make sure they know why the layer of fat is there (to ensure a beautifully cooked piece of expensive meat). They will not be disappointed, if they are, they're at the wrong party. Invite me next time.

2½ lb/1.2 kg boned and rolled loin of lamb
About 6 tbl Bronze Seasoning (p. 20)
6 tbl (3 oz/75 g) butter
1 cup (5 oz/125 g) finely chopped parsley

1 medium white onion, grated
1 tbl soy sauce
1 tbl Worcestershire Sauce
About 1 cup (8 fl oz/250 ml) wine or stock

Slice the lamb into noisettes in between the string loops it is tied with. Coat in bronze seasoning. Brown in a little butter. Remove and add chopped parsley and grated onion to pan, cook until onion is soft, add soy and Worcestershire Sauce. Loosen with a little wine or stock. Reduce to a near glaze.

Place noisettes on a grill pan, pour the glaze over them, and cook for 20 minutes, or for your desired temperature. Place 2-3 in center of the plate, ladle the Marchand de Vin Sauce over them. Serve side-orders separately.

Marchand de Vin Sauce

This is a popular sauce in the fancy restaurants of New Orleans. It is a strong wine sauce with mushrooms. In New Orleans, many places use ham as well as a very rich beef stock. I don't think most of us would have the real patience to make the necessary brown stock. But it is wonderful if you do.

3 cups (1 lb/450 g) mushrooms, finely chopped
1 medium onion, finely diced
3 1/2 oz/100 g butter
2 1/2 cups (1 pint/600 ml) beef stock
1 cup (8 fl oz/250 ml) red wine

1 tsp garlic salt
1 tsp coarse-ground black pepper
1 tsp cayenne
1 tbl dark roux (p. 21)

Sauté the mushroom and onion together in butter until soft, you may need or want to use a little of the stock to loosen the mixture. Remove from heat. Bring the stock to the boil, and add seasonings and roux. Simmer for 20-30 minutes. Add wine and onion mix, cook for a further 20 minutes. Check seasoning.

Cajun Meatloaf

This particular meatloaf is wild, excellent and extraordinary. I first ate Cajun Meatloaf at the Nellie Deli in New Orleans. Liz looked at me sideways when I ordered it. To her, it was square-shaped dog food. To me, at the time, it was everything America stood for.

As with Sheep Herder's Pie, cook Cajun meatloaf when you have excess or leftovers from other meat dishes. There are many gruesome tales about the ingredients in the mystery meatloaf and its gummy brown sauce. They are probably the vicious work of deranged veggies, but follow this recipe and you will discover meatloaf can be worth a detour.

It is above class distinctions, everyone should eat it. Unfortunately, not many restaurants in Britain sell it. So again, you will have to prepare it at home if you are going to try it. But as I mentioned earlier, home is the best place to eat anyways.

1 clove garlic, finely chopped
1 medium white onion, diced
1 medium red bell pepper, diced
6 rashers streaky bacon, chopped
1 cup (4 oz/125 g) mushrooms, coarsely diced
1 tbl Cajun seasoning (p. 19)
12 oz/300 g ground beef
3 cups (1 lb/450 g) ground pork

1 green jalapeño, diced
1 tbl creamed horseradish
1 cup (8 fl oz/250 ml) ketchup
3 scallions (spring onions), diced
1 cup (5 oz/125 g) seasoned breadcrumbs
2 eggs, beaten
1 tbl dry mustard

SERVES 4-6

Sauté garlic, onion and bell pepper in the butter for a few minutes. Add the bacon, mushrooms, and half of Cajun seasoning. Add meats and jalapeño, cook for 5 minutes. Keep stirring. Add a little stock if sticking. Cook until browned.

Remove from heat and fold in creamed horseradish, ketchup, scallions and breadcrumbs. Then mix in eggs, rest of seasoning and mustard. Transfer the mixture to a well-greased baking dish or your

Mom's Le Creuset terrine dish, cover, and bake at 350°F/180°C/gas mark 4 for about 1 hour. The meatloaf should be moist. If not, next time cook slower, check how lean the meats are, and add cream, or even creamed chicken soup.

To serve - nothing beats a brown gravy, mashed potatoes, and your favorite veggies. Comfort food at its best.

Cajun Sheep Herder's Pie

Now we have all eaten Shepherds Pie at school, right? If not, you are one of the lucky few. It is supposed to consist of finely chopped lamb with a potato crust. If only. Anyway this version will kill you, not that you'll find many sheep in the Bayou. Serve with cornmeal-fried okra and Ramona's Red Sauce, that is V-8 Juice, reduced with butter, red wine, Worcestershire Sauce and scallions.

You may wish to substitute sweet potatoes in place of the regular. If you do, add a little nutmeg and brown sugar to the pot when you boil. This helps give a more pronounced flavor.

1 medium onion, diced fine
4 cloves garlic, finely chopped
2 small red jalapeños
7 tbl (3½ oz/100 g) butter
2 cups (10 oz/250 g) finely chopped pork
2 cups (10 oz/250 g) finely chopped beef
3 cups (1 lb/450 g) cubed lamb
1 cup (5 oz/125 g) mushrooms, chopped
1 tsp cayenne
1 tsp garlic salt
1 tsp ground white pepper
1 tsp coarse-ground black pepper

1 tsp celery salt
½ cup (4 fl oz/125 ml) double cream
2 small yellow squash (marrows), peeled and
   sliced
1 medium green zucchini (courgette), peeled
   and sliced
3 medium carrots, sliced
1 medium red bell pepper
2 lb/1 kg mashed potato
2 tsp fresh thyme, chopped
½ cup (2½ oz/60 g) parsley, finely chopped
1 tbl onion powder

SERVES 4-6

Sauté onion, garlic, and jalapeños in half the butter, until onion is soft. Remove and add meats to pan; brown them, turning frequently. Put mushrooms and seasonings in a large bowl, mix them, then add browned meats and mix in. Add cream and mix again.

Transfer meat to baking dish. Mix zucchini and squash carrot, and bell pepper. Top meat with veggies.

Blend mashed potatoes with parsley, thyme, and onion powder and spread it over veggies. Dot with butter and bake for 2 hours at 350°F/180°C/gas mark 4.

Cornmeal-Fried Okra

3 cups (1 lb/450 g) okra, pods trimmed but left whole
1 cup (8 fl oz/250 ml) milk
1 egg, beaten
1 cup (5 oz/125 g) plain flour

1 cup (5 oz/125 g) cornmeal
1 tbl garlic salt
1 tbl paprika
2 cups (16 fl oz/500 ml) oil for deep-frying

Make a simple batter with milk, eggs and flour. Season cornmeal with garlic salt and paprika. Dip okra in batter then cornmeal. Repeat. Then fry until crispy.

Andouille-Stuffed Pork Tenderloin

This is a real winner of a dish. it is relatively easy to prepare and very professional looking. Serve on creamed potatoes and smother in gravy enriched with fat from the andouille. Pork tenderloin is a high grade, boneless cut taken from inside the loin of the pig.

3 pork tenderloins, trimmed and cut into
   2 in/5 cm medallions
3 andouille or smoked sausage links
2 cloves garlic, finely chopped
1 small red onion, grated
5 tbl (2½ oz/60 g) butter

1 tbl Worcestershire Sauce
1 tbl Louisiana Hot Sauce
1 tbl parsley, finely chopped
1 tbl plain flour
4 tbl olive oil

SERVES 4-6

Skin the sausages and break up the sausagemeat. Sauté the garlic and onion in butter, add Worcestershire sauce and hot sauce. After a few minutes, add sausage and cook until the sausage begins to leak its fat. Turn off heat and remove with a slotted spoon, you need the 'greeze' for the gravy. Mix parsley and flour with the sausagemeat. Let cool.

Push your finger into each cut of loin to make a hole, but do not break through to other side. Fill each one with andouille stuffing. Drizzle with olive oil and broil (grill) for 10 minutes or so, depending on how you like your meat cooked.

Pan-Fried Rabbit Tenderloin

This is hardly worth all the effort, unless you are using the rest of your rabbit or have rabbits from the Canary Islands. That said, rabbit tenderloins taste good.

Pan-fry the little babies in butter and fresh garlic, serve on steamed spinach and drizzle a little Creole mustard over the top. A nice O.T.T. starter.

If you have bought the whole lapin make a 'coq au vin' with it, they hold up great.

Jailhouse Chili

The dish called chili is serious. There are institutions all over the world dedicated to its cause. Surprising, when it is considered to be one of the few American originals. The origins are so vague I am not going to bother joining in a debate, especially as every nation has its own beef stew. Jailhouses and Firestations, in the States, produce some of the finest comfort foods. All that spare time and healthy appetites, I guess. Thus my chili's name.

Chuck steak is from the forequarter of the cow, between the neck and shoulder. It is very flavorful, but somewhat tough, thus ideal for chili-type stews. Please do not use store-bought chili mixes. Not even as your contribution to the village fête. Scary.

2 large yellow onions, diced
6 cloves garlic, finely chopped
6 tbl olive oil
3 tbl chili powder
5 medium red jalapeños, finely diced
2 lb/1 kg ground beef
1 lb/450 g chuck steak, cubed
6 rashers streaky bacon, diced and fried

2 tbl cumin
2 tbl oregano
1 tbl cayenne
1 tbl turmeric
2 cups (16 fl oz/500 ml) dark beer
2 cups (16 fl oz/500 ml) beef stock
5 cups (2½ lb/1.25 kg) plum tomatoes, crushed
2 tsp garlic salt

SERVES 6-8

Sauté onion and garlic in olive oil, after a few minutes add half the chili powder. Cook for a further 5 minutes add half of the diced jalapeños. In a mixing bowl, combine ground beef, chuck steak, bacon, the rest of the jalapeños and half the cumin, oregano, cayenne and turmeric. Mix well.

Add a cup (8 fl oz/250 ml) of beer to the onion, and as soon as it's hot, add the meats and brown, make sure all the contents of the mixing bowl are thrown in.

In a large pot, bring stock to boil with second half of the cumin, oregano, cayenne and oregano. Add tomatoes and meats. Only allow to simmer. After 1 hour add second half of chili seasoning and the garlic salt. Top up again with beer. Cook another hour or until beef is cooked.

Gravies

There are many ways to make gravy, I don't need to tell you that.

My favorite is Milk Gravy, where we mix flour and evaporated milk into the juices and debris resting at the bottom of a pan in which a roast chicken has been cooked. This is real Southern gravy. You can always cheat by using a stock reduction or by adding flavors to a blonde roux. The other general gravy I use is brown gravy. This time, beef debris is mixed with cornstarch (cornflour), red wine, beef stock, and seasoning. To make this into the red wine gravy, add brandy and port or sherry. Red-eye gravy is made from fried ham and black coffee.

The most important facet of gravies is the base you use. It has to be the result of cooking other items mixed with your favorite seasonings and a flour base to thicken and stretch, such as a roux.

Another favorite of mine is roast pecan gravy. Chicken stock forms the base, seasoned by a little soy sauce, Worcestershire Sauce, garlic salt, white pepper and scallions. A cup of pecans, that have been roasted in groundnut oil for 15 minutes, are added after the gravy has been removed from the heat.

SALADS

The Green Stuff

I am not a very good source of information on salads. However, I love making dressings. I use dressings for color and flavor, and not just for the salads. The greatest dressing exponent is Jean-Georges Vongerichten, who cooks in New York City. I strongly recommend you buy his book *Simple Cuisine*, Prentice-Hall, 1990. Excellent, beautiful, but far from simple.

At Kenny's we always had a type of side-salad on the menu called Junk Salad. This way I could play with the ingredients, for whatever reason. Basically it was a mixture of lettuces – oakleaf, radicchio, and lollo rosso – tossed with endive and a mixture of other raw vegetables, such as zucchini (courgettes), sweet peppers, red onions, and carrots. Various dressings were offered but Italian was the most popular. I cannot imagine you have never produced something similar at home. A similar salad to my Junk, found in the Crescent City and throughout the White Trash South, is the wonderfully, though rather disparagingly named Wop Salad. This is usually Romaine (cos) lettuce tossed with olives, artichokes, and anchovies and a few cooked vegetables. You may prefer to refer to it as Italian Salad.

'Italian' Dressing

I don't really know where this recipe comes from or why I called it Italian, thus the quotation marks, so maybe I should just call this Kenny's House Dressing, which it is. And can you believe, in over five years of passing it off as Italian in London, no-one mentioned it was an impostor! Never dress your lettuces too early, but make the dressing way in advance.

½ cup (4 fl oz/125 ml) olive oil
1 tbl white wine vinegar
1 small red onion, diced small

1 tsp garlic salt
1 tsp coarse-ground black pepper
1 tsp lemon juice

Combine the dressing ingredients. Keep chilled and shake well before use.

To make this into something closer to French dressing, add Dijon mustard. Crushed garlic is another nice addition (if a little strong) as is a couple of tablespoons of double cream. Creamy vinaigrette dressings are a visual delight, but only as long as the greens stay fresh. They soon absorb the dressing and become soggy.

Spiced Tomato Vinaigrette

¼ cup (2 fl oz/60 ml) red wine vinegar
¾ cup (6 fl oz/175 ml) olive oil
½ tsp coarse-ground black pepper
1 tsp sea salt

½ medium red onion, finely diced
1 medium red jalapeño, finely diced
1 small red bell pepper, finely diced
3 medium tomatoes, seeded

Blend all ingredients. Chill. Before use, bring to room temperature in a dark cupboard.

Blueberry Vinaigrette

1 cup (8 fl oz/250 ml) olive oil
⅓ cup (3 fl oz/75 ml) blueberry vinegar
1 tsp sea salt
1 tsp coarse-ground black pepper
1 cup (5 oz/125 g) blueberries

2 tbl olive oil
One orange, rind grated
1 pinch cinnamon
1 pinch nutmeg
2 tsp sugar

Combine the olive oil, blueberry vinegar, salt and pepper. Sauté blueberries in olive oil with rind, sugar, spices, and sugar for five minutes over high heat. Keep shaking. Cool. Add to the vinegar liquid and keep cool, preferably in the dark.

Hazelnut Dressing

3 tbl hazelnut oil

2 tbl light olive oil

2 tbl balsamic vinegar

1 small red onion, diced fine

1 tsp garlic salt

1 tsp coarse-ground black pepper

1 tbl hazelnuts, roasted, peeled, chopped small

Blend all ingredients.

Ranch Dressing

Once I had mastered it, Ranch Dressing became one of the most popular dressings, at least with the Americans. I refused to buy it in. That would have equated Kenny's with Long John Silver's or any of the other chain restaurants. Ranch is available in a few places in Britain. In the States, it is as nearly as ubiquitous as cocktail sauce and tartar sauce. The girls from Penn. State loved it when their tutors brought them in, so did Rex and his bar team.

2 cups (16 fl oz/500 ml) buttermilk

1 cup (8 fl oz/250 ml) mayonnaise

½ onion, grated

½ tbl Louisiana Hot Sauce

1 tbl lemon juice

1 tsp garlic powder

1 tsp garlic salt

1 tsp chives, finely chopped

1 tsp parsley, finely chopped

Blend all ingredients. You could cheat by simply mixing buttermilk with some sour cream and spices, but I never told you. Okay?

Blue Cheese Dressing

Some folk have tried to convince me that store-bought blue cheese dressing is best. Rubbish. Make my recipe and you will never try those insipid, sour efforts made by the conglomerates again. However, it may be too late and they already have your soul.

1 cup (5 oz/125 g) blue cheese, crumbled, at
*   room temperature (this allows the flavors to*
*   wake up)*
1 cup (8 fl oz/250 ml) sour cream (you can use
*   plain yogurt if you are a lazy shopper or live*
*   in the Canary Islands)*

1 tbl olive oil
1 tsp sugar
1 tbl lemon juice
1 tsp garlic salt
1 tsp ground white pepper
¹/₄ tsp paprika (optional)

Blend all ingredients. Don't chill before serving. Finely chopped parsley adds a little color and texture. Sprinkled paprika can also liven up presentation without taking away from the flavor.

Pecan Blue Balls

To the blue cheese dressing add cream cheese. Chill. Form into balls, then roll in chopped pecans, pressing hard so they inbed. They are an interesting appetizer or addition to a salad. A similar idea is to bake pecans in cheese-flavored pastry, for a fun party snack.

> *River Road Recipes* published by The Junior League of Baton Rouge, 1959, is a fine cookbook, until it talks of salads. Listen to this lot and you may begin to understand why I'd rather eat nothing but grilled guinea fowl thighs for the rest of my life: lime gelatin and cottage cheese salad, Coca-Cola salad, fruit and marshmallow salad, jellied guacamole salad, tomato soup salad (my favorite!)

The Caesar Salad

If I had to choose a salad to floor the rest, it would be old Cardini's! I usually serve Caesar salad as a side-order to Cajun Carbonara, or the other way around. Unless I make it a main course with the addition of meat such as Chicken Caesar or Grilled Shrimp Caesar.

The Caesar salad was created by Caesar Cardini, an Italian immigrant who became a bit of a big wheel in the restaurant community of Tijuana, near San Diego, just on the other side of the Mexican border. On July 4, 1924 he invented the salad. His version has no anchovies and only used Italian Parmesan and Italian olive oil.

Despite his successful patent application in 1948, do what you want. Cardini died in 1956. Please remember the International Society of Epicures in Paris once voted Caesar salad to be the greatest recipe to originate from America in fifty years. That says little for the rest of the Continent's cuisine or the Society.

Basically all you need is croutons, romaine (cos) lettuce, the dressing, and Parmesan cheese to garnish. I will leave the anchovies up to you, but if you were me....

To make croutons, use stale bread. Dice or cut into any shape, I prefer cutting a baguette into long strips. Lay them on a baking tray, sprinkle garlic salt and paprika over them, drizzle olive oil over, and bake for 20 minutes. Turn a few times and drain. Don't prepare too early.

Wash, dry, and tear up the lettuce as you feel fit.(I know, I don't have to tell you a knife will turn the edges brown fast). Allow up to one head per person, depending on whether the salad will be a starter or side-dish, and keep the pieces large. This allows for height in the presentation, plus your guests will take you for a generous soul. Keep chilled before tossing.

Nothing can beat freshly-grated Parmesan, please refrain from using the plastic variety.

Prepare dressing. In a large bowl toss the lettuce with most of the Parmesan, about $1/2$ cup ($2^1/2$ oz/ 60 g) per person. Add croutons and toss again. Add dressing and toss. Arrange on individual plates. Re-distribute the croutons - they fall to the bottom - and pour over any dressing left in the bowl. Garnish with a little extra cheese and anchovy fillets, if used. Please keep the lettuce high.

When executed properly, this salad will put a smile on the face of the unhappiest businessman. Trust me.

You could substitute arugula for the cos or romaine lettuce.

To really impress your guests, make croutons out of baguette rounds and top each one with sautéed rounds of soft goat's cheese. Sear the cheese quickly in olive oil or hazelnut oil with fresh herbs such as thyme or rosemary. You could also garnish with eggplant chips or caramelized halved shallots.

Caesar Dressing

1 cup (8 fl oz/250 ml) olive oil	3 egg yolks
$1/4$ cup ($2^1/2$ fl oz/60 ml) white wine vinegar	1 tsp coarse-ground black pepper
$1/4$ cup ($2^1/2$ fl oz/60 ml) lemon juice	1 tsp garlic salt
1 tsp Worcestershire Sauce	6 anchovy fillets

Blend the whole lot together. If a frothy head is kicking off, it's because you let some egg white in - you were lazy. You'd better stop, unless you want Caesar Meringue!

If you are worried about using raw egg yolks, maybe coddle them first. This should make enough for 4-6 salads.

Cajun Carbonara

A very popular pasta dish in the Italian home, usually made with bacon. I prefer to funk it up with tasso – our spicy, smoky ham (see p. 149) and of course jalapeños. I find it strange that Italian cooking is devoid of strong spicing.

To serve Carbonara with a Caesar salad is fun, but it also makes an excellent full meal and is encouragingly home-made-looking. You will soon appreciate the interaction. Leave the pasta in a large serving bowl and let your guests help themselves.

1 medium white onion, grated
1 cup (5 oz/125 g) tasso, diced fine
1 medium green jalapeño, finely diced
5 tbl (2½ oz/60 g) butter
1 tsp ground white pepper
1 tsp onion salt

1 cup (8 fl oz/250 ml) red wine
9 oz/300 g cooked spaghetti
½ cup (4 fl oz/125 ml) cream
5 egg yolks, beaten
½ cup (2½ oz/60 g) Parmesan cheese

MAKES 4 SIDE ORDERS

Sauté tasso, onion, and jalapeño in butter. Add seasoning and wine, after 5 minutes add pasta and cream, heat through. Remove from heat and mix in yolks. Return to heat and add Parmesan. Mix and serve.

Blackened Chicken Salad
with Creole Vinaigrette

Along with Junk salad, Blackened Chicken Salad remained on our menu for years. It is actually very good for a contrived invention. Most of my creations seem to be born of 'déshabille.' It is very important to top the salad with the meats and serve immediately, as the salad stuff will wilt very fast under the heat.

The key is to serve the meats straight from the pan and the salad straight from the refrigerator.

3 tbl cider vinegar	1 tsp garlic salt
8 tbl olive oil	1 tsp ground white pepper
2 tsp coarse-ground mustard	1 tsp parsley, finely chopped
2 shallots, finely chopped	1 tsp lemon juice

Mix the ingredients in the order given. Pour the mixture into a screwtop jar and close tightly. Store in a cool, dark place or the refrigerator.

Another easy combination - a blackened chicken supreme (or breast), sliced whilst still hot and served on top of a dressed Junk salad, though the veggies have to be much neater and thinner than for a regular junk. Toss the salad in the vinaigrette first and serve straight away so the salad does not become either soggy or wilted under the heat from the chicken. Obviously, you can play with the idea and serve other blackened meats on the salad. We also did a successful Blackened Shrimp Salad.

Shrimp Remoulade

This salad is effectively New Orleans equivalent of the prawn cocktail. If you have good-quality shrimp it can be excellent. If not, pass on it, just as you do for this classic appetizer served in every pub or steakhouse in Britain. Remoulade sauce is divine but there are better uses for it. This dish needs good presentation and an interesting selection of dressed lettuces. NEVER USE ICEBERG.

About 1 lb/450 g raw jumbo shrimp

2½ cups (1 pint/600 ml) fish stock, clamato juice (p. 22), or V-8 juice

1 tbl 3-way pepper seasoning (equal quantities, of cayenne, black pepper, and paprika)

1 tbl garlic salt

1 tbl Remoulade Sauce (p. 93)

4 lettuces, tossed and dressed

1 red onion, diced

1 tbl Louisiana Hot Sauce

Cook the shrimp freshly in fish stock, clamato, or V-8 juice. Add garlic salt and 3-way pepper seasoning to the poaching liquid. Cool the shrimp, retain the liquid for another dish. Place the Remoulade sauce in the middle of a small plate, cover in dressed lettuces.

Toss the shrimp in diced red onion and hot sauce. Place on the lettuces. Serve.

Andouille and Bean Salad

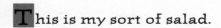

This is my sort of salad.

Slices of andouille, baked or grilled and cooled soaked in water overnight

Fresh black beans

Black-eyed peas

Red beans

2½ cups (1 pint/600 ml) chicken stock

2 garlic cloves, chopped

3 cups (1 lb/450 g) fresh haricot beans

1 red onion, sliced very thin

2 green jalapeños, very finely diced

'Italian' dressing (p. 180)

Cook the beans together in the chicken stock and garlic for an hour or until soft. Drain and cool. Top and tail the haricot beans and boil them in water to cover for 10 minutes. Drain and cool. Toss the beans with rest of the ingredients and serve.

House Potato Salad

2 lb/900 g small potatoes
3 rashers streaky bacon
2 tbl olive oil
1 small green bell pepper, diced fine
3 hard-boiled eggs, chopped

1 small white onion, quarters sliced
1 cup mayonnaise
½ tbl coarse-ground black pepper
½ tbl garlic salt
Juice of 1 lemon

Boil the potatoes until tender, then slice them into about 5 pieces each. Dice the bacon and fry it in the olive oil. Combine with the rest of the ingredients

I prefer my potato salads warm. So I mix all the ingredients into the mayonnaise and add the potatoes as soon as they are ready. You may wish to leave it in the refrigerator to chill. Somehow I don't think we would live together in harmony.

ALL THE POTATO SALADS SERVE 4-6 FOLK AS A SIDE ORDER

Garage Potato Salad

2 lb/900 g small potatoes
½ cup (2½ oz/60 g) celery, diced real fine
1 small white onion, grated
1 cup (8 fl oz/250 ml) mayonnaise
1 tbl dry mustard
1 tsp white wine vinegar
1 tsp ground white pepper

1 tsp celery salt
1 small red jalapeño, diced fine
½ cup (2½ oz/60 g) sweet pickles, diced
½ cup (2½ oz/60 g) green olives, coarsely
   chopped
1 tbl parsley, finely chopped

Boil the potatoes until tender, then slice them into about 5 pieces each. Mix with the rest of the ingredients as before, or as you see fit.

My Fishing Potato Salad

This takes its name from the ham and peas, which I once appropriated to use for bait on a particularly barren fishing trip.

2 lb/1 kg small potatoes
1 small white onion, grated
2 small green jalapeños, finely diced
1 cup (8 fl oz/250 ml) mayonnaise
3 scallions (springonions), cut into thirds

1 cup (5 oz/125 g) sharp Cheddar cheese, grated
2 links smoked sausage, grilled and sliced
1 cup (5 oz/125 g) smoked ham, diced
1 cup (5 oz/125 g) black-eyed peas, cooked and
   rinsed

Boil the potatoes until tender, then coarsely chop them. Mix with the rest of the ingredients as before, or as you see fit. There is enough seasoning without adding salt or pepper.

Coleslaw

'I fought the slaw and the slaw won'

I have never been a fan of coleslaw, although I like the flavor of coleslaw dressing. In the first restaurant where I worked, coleslaw was simply red and white cabbage mixed with a dressing consisting of religiously-prepared mayonnaise, sugar, lemon juice, and sour cream. Numerous versions exist. Besides my recipe, other ingredients, such as mustard, apples, potatoes, pickle, bacon, ginger, and even pineapple, have found their way into coleslaw. I don't really care what you do.

½ small head white cabbage, shredded
½ small head red cabbage, shredded
1 small white onion, grated
1 cup (5 oz/125 g) carrots, grated
1 cup (8 fl oz/250 ml) mayonnaise

½ cup (2½ oz/60 g) sugar
1 cup (8 fl oz/250 ml) sour cream
1 tbl white wine vinegar
1 tsp sea salt
1 tsp coarse-ground black pepper

SERVES 4-6 AS A SIDE ORDER

Mix white and red cabbage with carrot. Add salt and pepper, chill. Mix other ingredients together. When ready for serving mix together well.

Cool-Slaw

1 tbl olive oil
4 cups (1¼ lb/500 g) white cabbage, shredded
1 cup (4 oz/125 g) red onion, sliced
1 medium green bell pepper, diced very small
1 tbl dry mustard

1 tsp celery salt
2 tbl white wine vinegar
4 rashers streaky bacon, chopped and grilled
1 red apple, cored and diced

Mix the oil into the cabbage and add onion, pepper and chill. Mix mustard and celery salt into vinegar, add bacon and apple. Combine all just before serving.

Chow-Chow

A southern style of coleslaw I do like, however, is Chow-Chow. In some parts of the South, it 's their version of 'slaw. Chow-Chow is a Southern relish with pickled cabbage, green tomatoes, onions, chiles, and sweet peppers. We cook our version.

191

3 cups (1 lb/450 g) tomatoes, skinned, de-seed
   and chopped
1 large white onion
3 cups (1 lb/450 g) green tomatoes, chopped
1 cup (5 oz/125 g) red cabbage, chopped small
2 medium red bell peppers, finely chopped
1 red jalapeño, finely chopped
1½ cups (8 oz/200 g) sugar

1 tsp cayenne
1 tsp garlic salt
1 tsp allspice
1 tsp mace
1 tsp paprika
½ cup (4 fl oz/125 ml) oil
2 cups (16 fl oz/500 ml) red wine vinegar

Mix all ingredients, except vinegar; sauté in oil. Cover with vinegar, simmer for 10-15 minutes. Cool.
Pour into screwtop jars and seal.

BRUNCH

A Sunday Morning Tale

'Heavenly Father
From the abundance of Your streams, fields, and earth
You have seen fit to bless our table
and we are grateful.
We pray for your constant guidance in all things
and let us never forget
to give thanks for the way
You have blessed the hands of the cook.'

Amen

Food in the South is given a high level of respect which goes back many years, regardless of how humble the food is. It is often referred to as 'soul food' or food cooked 'soulfully.' Recipes were passed down from generation to generation and the whole family would be found sitting around the table sharing whatever the table had to offer.

Brunch is a portmanteau word – look it up, I had to! – and I'm not referring to a leather case. It combines breakfast and lunch. According to *Punch* in 1896, the word was introduced in the previous year by a guy called Beringer, in the *Hunters Weekly*. It referred to a meal consumed after a morning hunting trip. In the States, now it is big news, particularly on Sundays in hotels and restaurants. In Britain it is slowly catching on.

Brunch is a wonderful invention, a perfect setting for hungover fathers and uncles to be annoyed by younger members of the clan. Bloody Marys are of course an integral part of a satisfactory brunch, but equally important are fresh flowers, glasses of Kir Royale, Mimosas, and good company. But the most important ingredients are fresh eggs, Hollandaise sauce, tomato salsa, and English muffins.

English Muffins

These are actually muffins eaten in the U.S., based on the traditional English version, and so called because in the U.S. a muffin without the English is a sort of cup-cake. They are round, flattish scones, made from the usual bread ingredients, with added malted barley and semolina. In Britain we don't do this. Historians say the name (English) comes from S.B. Thomas & Co. of New York. A company founded by an English guy back in 1880. They pioneered this type of muffin, or so we are told.

Anyway they are wonderful, much better than croissants, but just don't try and make them yourself. Store-bought are best – funny how a few things are like that.

Hollandaise

Hollandaise sauce is a must for any successful brunch and it may help to produce a batch before the invites are sent out. It also has the ability to make your mascara run.

What you do is nearly cook the eggs. You will soon realize if they have cooked completely as you will be left with a funny sort of, unappetizing scrambled egg.

This first version is not mine, but it's a fool proof version from Louisiana. For both methods you will need a double boiler – this helps to keep the cooking slow.

Louisiana-style

1 cup (8 fl oz/250 ml) water heated over a double boiler, with your favorite seasonings and lemon juice added.

Mix 1 tablespoon of cornstarch (cornflour) with a little water, add to water and mix until thick. Remove from heat.

Beat 3 egg yolks, add cornstarch mix to egg yolks with one big tablespoon of butter. Place over heat and cook until thick again. Before serving, a little more butter may help.

My style

8 egg yolks	1 tsp parsley, finely chopped
1 tsp garlic salt	3 tbl (1 1/2 oz/40 g) melted butter
1 tsp cayenne	1 tbl double cream

Season the yolks with salt and cayenne and add the parsley. In the top half of a double boiler, beat the yolks while drizzling in the butter. Add a little lemon juice and the cream. Keep stirring, and add a dash of white wine vinegar. When ready leave there, but turn off heat until needed.

Scrambled Eggs

The key to scrambled eggs is to remove the pan from the direct heat way before you think they are finished. Never scrape the pan or mix 'hard,' just keep folding.

I enjoy adding a little color to the egg mix, like diced chives and finely diced, well prepared red chiles.

Poached Eggs

Poach eggs in boiling water to which you have added either a little vinegar or lemon juice. The acidity speeds up coagulation of the egg whites and generally gives the egg a decent shape. Don't crack the eggs early, wait for the water to nearly reach boiling point, then crack the egg onto a small plate and slide into the water. The effort is worth it. Please don't think you are Paul Newman and just use one hand. If the egg fails to perform, it is probably not fresh, not entirely your fault. The same applies to frying eggs – but who fries eggs any more?

Pancakes

Pancakes rarely break out of the basic flour – butter – milk format. For some that is fine. As with most items however, I quickly became bored and played around, adding fruits, flavors, alcohol, and different bases.

One such creation was my Holiday Pancakes, created on an Easter Sunday. Using cornmeal instead of flour, I opened up whole new vistas – flavorful and colorful. Many traditionalists were confused when their expected light and fluffy creations had not arrived. (They only had to ask.)

All the literature I have read about pancakes is full of caveats on the subject, such as 'stir with soft touch', 'stroke lightly,' 'mix until just blended,' and so on. What they are all trying to say is: do not beat up the batter, you WANT lumps. Beating develops gluten, which creates a network of strong elastic fibers. That's fine for bread but it screws up pancakes. Other factors will also affect the results, such as age of the flour, but that applies to all recipes.

Holiday Pancakes will be slow to absorb milk, so make them a little earlier than you would regular ones. Whatever style you choose will not detract from the fact that pancakes for breakfast are a real winner.

You may feel you will not have the time to make them due to your busy, demanding lifestyle, so make them at weekends. Nothing sets off a nice day better than hot coffee, cold juice, fruit, syrups and the smell of fresh pancakes.

Conversely, there is nothing worse than having to make a batter for hundreds of pancakes when you are suffering from 'kitchen fatigue' or handling an order for a special customer – such as blackened, 'not on the Brunch menu' steak – when the griddle is full of blueberry pancakes, buttermilk pancakes, and holiday pancakes. Spicy flapjacks anyone?

Pancakes are usually served in stacks of three.

You will ideally need a griddle, but it is possible to improvize by using a thick, wide frying pan. Note: we are not making crêpes.

American Pancakes

1½ cups (8 oz/200 g) plain flour
½ tsp salt
5 tsp sugar
2 tsp baking powder
2 eggs, separated

1 cup (8 fl oz/250 ml) milk
About 2 cups (16 fl oz/500 ml) maple syrup
Fresh fruit, to serve (optional)
8 tbl icing sugar, sifted (optional)

Mix lightly dry ingredients. Beat the yolks and combine with the milk, then add dry ingredients. Beat the whites until stiff and gently fold into the liquid. Decide on size and thickness of pancake you fancy. Drop tablespoon amounts onto your lightly buttered griddle.

The pancakes are ready as soon as each side is a nice brown. Stack high on each other and serve with maple syrup dripping over them. Fresh fruit garnishes look cool, as does icing sugar on top of the syrup.

Blueberry Pancakes

Make as before, but add a little extra milk and a pinch of cinnamon. If you use frozen berries, drain them first, but try and find fresh, though bruise them first. 1 cup (5 oz/125 g) will do fine, add them before the egg white stage. Other fruits also work well, providing they are in small pieces. Peach pancakes sold well.

Pigs in Blankets

Wrap a pancake around a hot sausage, smother in maple syrup, and enjoy. Born from a desperate need for energy, 2 minutes before service - though not by me!

Holiday Pancakes

1 cup (5 oz/125 g) cornmeal (not cornflour)
1/2 cup (2 1/2 oz/60 g) plain flour
1/2 tsp salt
2 tsp baking powder
1/2 tsp bicarbonate of soda
2 scallions (spring onions), finely chopped
1 tbl red bell pepper, finely chopped

1 tsp red jalapeño, chopped very fine
1 tbl sweetcorn kernels
1/2 tsp salt
3 eggs, beaten
About 1 1/4 cups (10 fl oz/300 ml) buttermilk (or milk if it is not available)
Butter for griddle

MAKES 4-6 SERVINGS

Mix dry ingredients, then, separately, mix vegetables and add salt to them.

Beat eggs with the milk. Then fold in dry mix, do not beat hard. Add vegetables. Leave for a few minutes, the mixture may need more milk.

Cook as normal for pancakes giving them about 1 1/2 minutes on each side. The butter should give a golden color. Poke with a toothpick or fork, if it comes out clean, they are ready. Diced crispy bacon is a an alternative which you could add.

Muffins

Home-baked muffins are marvelous in their simplicity. You would be a fool to think they are beyond you. They are easier than scrambled eggs. Trust me. Can you imagine their delight when you pull out of the oven, your own made tray of pecan muffins. A very satisfying start to the day.

American muffin pans are deeper than English patty pans or bun tins. You should be able to find them at a good cookware store. Otherwise bake them in the paper cases used for cup-cakes.

1 cup (5 oz/125 g) sugar
5 tbl (2½ oz/ 60 g) melted butter
2 eggs
½ cup (4 fl oz/125 ml) buttermilk, plain yogurt,
*   or milk*

2 cups (10 oz/250 g) plain flour
1 tsp baking powder
1 cup (5 oz/125 g) chopped pecans

MAKES 12 MUFFINS

Heat oven to 375°F/190°C/gas mark 5. Grease a 12-cup muffin pan. Mix sugar, melted butter, and eggs. Stir in half a cup of buttermilk or plain yogurt or milk. Separately, combine the flour, baking powder and pecans (or whatever filling you fancy - blueberries are a favorite) and slowly stir this into the liquid. Portion into greased muffin cups, bake for 30 minutes max.

French Toast

Many folk like to use regular sliced bread for these toasts. I suggest you use slices of baguette. Much funkier. Do not use fresh bread, no real need, as the milk batter needs to soak into the bread. The milk will find it harder the fresher the bread. If you only have fresh bread, leave out to dry for a few hours, or overnight.

3 eggs, beaten
1 cup (8 fl oz/250 ml) milk
3 tbl Grand Marnier, Triple Sec, or orange juice
1 tbl sugar
Grated zest of one lemon
Grated zest of half an orange

½ tsp of vanilla essence
12 thick, 2 in/5 cm slices baguette
Butter for frying
1 tbl cinnamon, for garnish
Fresh fruit for garnish

SERVES 4

Beat the ingredients lightly and pour the batter over the baguettes. Let the bread soak up the batter for 10-15 minutes. Fry 3 minutes on each side.

Garnish with maple syrup, cinnamon, and fresh fruit. (Were you aware that counterfeiting cinnamon used to be a seriously lucrative trade, all because the authentic spice was so expensive?)

If you feel like being real fancy, in true Louisiana fashion, stuff your French Toast. With peaches or sliced strawberry's.

Pain Perdue – Lost Bread – Spanish Toast

'Lost bread' is Creole-speak for stale bread. Hopefully, the baguette will be yesterday's, if not leave out for a while.

12 2-inch/5 cm thick slices of baguette
2 eggs
2 cups (16 fl oz/500 ml) milk
4 tsp white sugar
1 tsp vanilla essence

2 tsp brandy
About 6 tbl (3 oz/75 g) butter for frying
4 tbl icing sugar to garnish
Fresh fruit to garnish

SERVES 4

Mix all ingredients together well, except bread, icing sugar and fruit. Soak bread in batter for 10-15 minutes. Slowly fry in butter until crisp on outside. Garnish with confectionery sugar and fruit.

201

One way to really lose your 'pain perdue,' is to cut it into small pieces, toast it, and mix into scrambled eggs.

The Monte Cristo Breakfast Sandwich

Make a ham and cheese sandwich, soak in a French toast batter, made without the sugar, and fry. You bet!

Beignets

When produced correctly Beignets are heavenly. More often than not, though, they are a dreadful embarrassment. I know. I have screwed up thousands of them. Beignet (ben-YEY) is French for fritter, a puffy, yeasty, deep-fried pastry, which is traditionally served at breakfast smothered in icing sugar.

The finest place to taste beignets on the planet, has to be the Café du Monde in the French Quarter of New Orleans. They serve them 24 hours a day, 365 days a year. They are wonderful. Despite having a sack of their beignet mix sent over, I still never managed to create anything near to their beignets, which are all regular, light, fluffy and rectangular. Mine usually resembled cosmic explosions! I guess the key is in producing a dough which you can roll out into the exact shapes required. Best of luck.

This is the real recipe, be careful it might work.

¼ cup sugar

2 tbl shortening (cooking fat)

¼ tsp salt

½ cup (4 fl oz/125 ml) boiling water

½ cup (4 fl oz/125 ml) evaporated milk

½ sachet dry yeast

4 tbl warm water

1 egg beaten

3½ cups (17½ oz/500 g) plain flour

About 2 cups (16 fl oz/500 ml) oil for frying

MAKES ABOUT 24 FRITTERS

Start yesterday. In a mixing bowl, place sugar, shortening, and salt; mix well. add boiling water to the mix and stir well. Dissolve yeast in lukewarm water. Let it bubble in a warm place.

Add evaporated milk to egg, mix and add to yeast. Add 2 cups (10 oz/250 g) of the flour to the milk batter. Keep adding flour until you have a soft dough. Refrigerate until tomorrow.

Roll into the dough until it is 5 in/13 cm thick, cut into 2 in/5 cm squares and deep-fry in oil at 350°F/180°C until golden-brown. Try a couple first before adding a bigger batch. Drain on kitchen paper when done and cover in powdered sugar

Ideally serve with café au lait, New Orleans style. This is coffee, water and milk boiled together, add chicory to be real authentic.

Hash

Hash refers to a breakfast dish of chopped ingredients, usually including potatoes. I tried various combinations and found chicken, salmon, and crab the best. Sometimes I traded sweet potatoes for regular. My favorite is Red Flannel Hash, which combines corned beef and pickled beetroots. The name derives from the French to chop, 'hacher' and is usually associated with cheap foods, served in diner-type establishments. The best known hash is corned beef hash, sometimes called 'corn beef Willie,' don't ask me why.

House Hash

5 large white potatoes
6 tbl (3 oz/75 g) butter
1 medium white onion, grated
1 medium red jalapeño, diced fine
1 tsp sea salt

1 tsp garlic salt
2 tsp ground white pepper
1 tbl soy sauce
2 cups (10 oz/250 g) mushrooms, chopped

Boil the potatoes and coarsely chop them or cut into semi-circles. (I prefer the skins left on, a flavor thing, but to be a little more sophisticated you may want to remove them.) Heat the butter in a large, heavy-based frying pan, and sauté onion and jalapeño with sea salt. Add the potatoes and brown them. Add garlic salt and white pepper, keep cooking add soy sauce and mushrooms. Turn off heat and keep mixing. Remove to serving platter and keep warm in oven. This basic house hash is good for a side-order, plate garnish, or a meal on its own, topped with eggs.

Corn Beef Hash

To the above hash add 1½ cups (8 oz/200 g) corned beef, Worcestershire Sauce, and diced, red bell pepper. An adaptation on this is to save the leftovers from a roast beef joint, with some debris and gravy, and make a roast beef hash.

Red Flannel Hash

To the corned beef hash add 2 cups (8 oz/250 g) diced but not drained, pickled beetroot. Then slice 4 rashers streaky bacon into 3 in/7 cm strips and fry it until crisp. Add to the hash.

Salmon Hash

To the House Hash, add coarsely chopped, raw, fresh salmon with maybe a couple of tablespoons of clamato juice. Add the fish just before the hash is ready.

Full House Hash

Add grilled andouille slices, tasso, and steak trimmings to the House Hash.

Chicken Liver Hash

Dice the livers and add just before the hash has finished.

'Hash Browns' are nothing like hash, although the same preparation principle applies. They are essentially a deep- or pan-fried potato fritter. My favorite version is grated potato, mixed with onion and bacon, then fried in butter until crisp. Commercially, they are deep-fried, but you will not find many breakfast cooks doing that.

Home Fries

To find two Americans from two different States to agree on what Home Fries are, is impossible. This is my version from the 51st State.

2 lb/1 kg medium potatoes, unpeeled and boiled
1 medium white onion, sliced
2 scallions (spring onions), chopped
1 cup (4 oz/125 g) mushrooms
5 tbl (2½ oz/60 g) butter
½ medium red jalapeño, diced fine

1 tbl soy sauce
1 cup (5 oz/125 g) Cheddar cheese, grated
1 tsp sea salt
1 tsp ground white pepper
Parsley, finely chopped for garnish

Slice the potatoes thickly or quarter them. Sauté the onions, scallions, and mushrooms. Add potatoes, and cook until brown. Add jalapeño and seasoning, soy sauce, and maybe a little of water to loosen. Cook for a further 5-10 minutes.

Just before serving loosely mix in the cheese. Garnish with parsley.

Eggs Benedict

This is the most popular restaurant brunch item. It is traditionally served with Canadian bacon. I prefer ham. I feel the ham in Britain is better than what they have Stateside – I hear the Virginians screaming already.

The English muffin is vital, as is the Hollandaise Sauce (p. 195), to produce an authentic Benny. The dish is ridiculously simple to assemble, but it relies on your poaching ability, particularly if you are cooking for more than four. If you are proficient, expect some groovy dinner invites. If not, hope your Bloody Marys are slowly anesthetizing your guests.

As with all my brunch dishes I like to garnish Benny's with tomato salsa (p. 25).

Despite always being associated with 'Breakfast at Brennans' – Brennans in New Orleans – the dish originates up in New York City. It happened at the legendary Delmonico's Restaurant, where one day the maître d'hotel helped a couple of bored regulars choose their own brunch. Their names were Mr & Mrs Le Grand Benedict. They came up with something a little different. The name Benedict first appeared in print in 1928 and has nothing to do with a blessing.

8 eggs
4 English muffins
8 thick slices smoked ham,

1 cup (8 fl oz/250 ml) Hollandaise sauce (p. 195)
½ cup (2½ oz/60 g) parsley, finely chopped
Tomato Salsa (p. 25) for garnish

SERVES 4

Poach the eggs, they must be very well drained, soggy muffins are the worst. Split and toast the muffins. Grill the ham just before serving. Put the ham on the muffin and sit the eggs on top, then smother in Hollandaise and sprinkle with parsley.

You will have to think up your own names for variations, but I once substituted the Hollandaise with an apple cider cream sauce. It appealed to my less-than-hearty appetite, Hollandaise is very filling. One guy I know orders a bowl of Hollandaise and a portion of fries for his brunch.

In some Southern restaurants Potatoes O'Brien are the standard Benny garnish. These are Home Fries, smothered in sweated onions and bell peppers.

Bloody Mary

Kenny's became renowned for it's Bloodys. More of a meal than a drink.

At the side Bar of Arnauds, the ephemereal and late Herman garnished his Bloodys with pickled asparagus. I loved watching this proud old gentleman serving the rich locals of New Orleans. Despite being a fishing rod's distance off Bourbon Street the 'messy' tourists never found it. Check it out. I usually garnish with celery, as does everyone. But that's Okay.

2 pint V-8 juice. Nothing else will do. NOTHING!
(it is tomato and vegetable juice made by
Campbells)
1 tbl creamed horseradish
1 tbl coarse grained mustard
1 tsp Worcestershire Sauce

2 tsp Louisiana Hot Sauce
1 tbl lemon juice
1 tsp sea salt
1 tsp cayenne
1 tsp coarse-ground black pepper

Mix well and chill overnight.

If you prefer gin to vodka, make a Bloody Louis, tequila - Bloody Maria, Saki - Bloody Mary Quite Contrary, no alcohol - Bloody Shame, just joking it's called a Virgin Mary. Get the picture?

Eggs Crawkitty

(My angel of compassion)

I cannot remember where I first saw this dish, but I do hold my hands up in the air and apologize to whoever invented it, for copying it and even at times claiming it to be mine. It consists of poached eggs riding on a grilled catfish fillet, smothered in a crawfish Hollandaise. In my opinion, it is the best brunch item I ever cooked. Ignoring the price, it is a winner. Maybe you should save its mysteries for your wedding morning. My extra touch of sautéeing the crawfish tails in garlic, jalapeños, and butter adds a little of my own style, but not a whole lot.

4 catfish fillets
4 tbl olive oil
1 lemon, juice squeezed
2 tbl soy sauce
1 tbl garlic salt
1 clove garlic, finely chopped
4 scallions (spring onions)
5 tbl (2¹/₂ oz/60 g) butter

¹/₂ medium red jalapeño, finely diced
1 cup (8 oz/250 g) crawfish tails
1 tsp coarse-ground black pepper
8 eggs
2 cups (16 fl oz/500 ml) Hollandaise sauce
  (p. 195)
Parsley, finely chopped

SERVES 4

Marinate the catfish for 2 hours in olive oil, lemon juice, soy sauce and garlic salt. Grill the marinated catfish, use the oil to baste in grilling. Cook slowly. Meanwhile, sauté garlic and scallions in butter, after 3 minutes add jalapeños and crawfish. Turn off heat and add pepper. Poach the eggs.

Top each catfish fillet with two eggs, then crawfish, and then Hollandaise. Garnish with parsley. Sublime. Go to the local bar and celebrate.

Grillades and Grits

There is no recipe here for grillades and grits (gree-odds), but I anticipated criticism if I ignored this dish. Today, the dish usually consists of braised veal steaks. It should be the lean of the sow's belly, the thin meat strips running through the thick belly section of a pig.

Grits are hominy kernels ground and cooked, a bit like porridge in taste. They are a Southern staple but I'm no fan of either. If offered grits, ask for them buttered, garlic, or cheesy, anything but plain.

Huevos Rancheros

This is not by any means a real Southern dish, more an import from the border territories. However, along with Eggs Benedict, it is, for many Americans, synonymous with the brunch meal. The name means ranch-style eggs, I will not help you to pronounce it, consequently leaving it open to your own interpretation.

As vague as its name suggests, Huevos Rancheros can be prepared in a variety of ways. I have various adaptations, such as adding black beans, blue corn tortillas, and feta cheese, and there are versions with no beans, just red chili sauce and Monterey Jack cheese (tastes like a very sharp Cheddar). One version I prepare at home is re-fried black beans, topped with cilantro, and red pepper-flavored scrambled eggs.

The dish basically calls for flour tortillas, eggs, and re-fried pinto beans. Flour tortillas (NOT to be confused with corn tortilla chips) can now be found in most of the major supermarket chains. The rest is up to you really. Always chop the jalapeños real fine, otherwise they will only hurt people and not add to the general flavor of the dish.

4 flour tortillas, slightly warmed

2 cups (10 oz/250 g) pinto beans, soaked
    overnight in water to cover, and drained

3 cups (1¼ pints/ 750 ml) stock

½ cup (2½ oz/60 g) ham, finely chopped
    (optional)

4 eggs

2 tbl (1 oz/25 g) butter or 2 tbl oil

1 cup (8 fl oz/250 ml) tomato salsa (p. 25)

2 red jalapeños, very finely chopped

½ cup (4 fl oz/125 ml) sour cream

To make re-fried pinto beans, cook the pinto beans in the stock with seasoning, garlic, and onion. Cook until soft, then mash and re-heat or fry; I use ham in the prep. Poach the eggs. Spread the beans over the tortilla and top with the eggs and salsa, then garnish with sour cream and jalapeños. Some restaurants use hash brown potatoes instead of beans, sounds good huh?

Eggs Lafitte

Jean Lafitte was a villainous pirate who became a local hero in New Orleans. He used to terrorize the waters around the mouth of the Mississippi until the British attempted to colonize the area. At the Battle of New Orleans, in 1815, Lafitte and his men fought beside General Andrew Jackson and helped defeat the British 'invaders' – consequently working his way into the heart of all New Orleans folk.

This has a similar derivation to dishes like Eggs Basin Street and Salmon Hash. Eggs Lafitte, however, remained on the menu perennially and consistently sold out.

A real Kenny's classic, it consists of sautéed tomato rounds and grilled crabcakes (see p. 78) on English muffins with poached eggs and Hollandaise sauce.

Crabmeat in breakfast cooking is not new. There are many examples of its use as in crab hash and crabmeat omelette, but I could never come up with anything more exciting than Eggs Lafitte. Enjoy.

8 crabcakes

8 slices tomato

8 poached eggs

4 English muffins, toasted

5 tbl (2¹/₂ oz/60 g) butter

Hollandaise Sauce (p. 195)

Parsley, finely chopped or mock black caviar to garnish

SERVES 4

Very simple. Sauté crabcakes in butter, remove and keep warm. Sauté tomatoes in same pan. Build dish and garnish. If you substitute sautéed sea-trout for the crabcakes, you have Eggs Clare - pretty name.

Eggs Maw Maw

I have seen the name Maw Maw attached to a few dishes, so I used it too. It probably is a play on Mamou. The rice in this dish has to be thoroughly drained, otherwise it leaks and that's messy.

6 tbl (3 oz/75 g) cooked ham

6 tbl (3 oz/75 g) peeled shrimp

1 small onion, grated

¹/₂ cup (4 fl oz/125 ml) orange juice

3 cups (1 lb/450 g) cooked rice

2 tsp sea salt

1 tsp coarse-ground black pepper

3 eggs

1 orange, thinly sliced, for garnish

4 tbl parsley, finely chopped for garnish

Sauté cooked ham with shrimp and grated onion, mix in orange juice. Add cooked rice, warm through, add a little sea salt and coarsely ground black pepper. Beat eggs together then scramble with shrimp mix. Garnish with twisted orange slices and parsley.

Kenny's Steak 'n' Eggs

Very much diner food, but glorious in execution. There are many ways to present this dish. Basically you either grill the steak as normal, and throw eggs on top. Or you try and produce another dish worthy of pre-fixing with your own name, such as 'Bubba's Steak 'n' Eggs.'

I produce a sauté of vegetables, a sauté of potatoes, onions, and mushrooms. I marinade the steak in soy sauce, onion and hot sauce, then grill to just under the desired temperature, slice, then flash-fry with the other ingredients. The whole gallimaufry is topped with eggs – cook them your way – then smothered in a Bordelaise sauce. 'Kenny's Steak 'n' Eggs.'

Eggs Basin Street

Born out of an over-exuberance in the previous day's red bean preparation. It is a nice way to serve eggs, despite its appeal being largely restricted to 'big' eaters or Southern folk. Just top a plate of Red Beans (see p. 36) with poached eggs, garnish with chopped scallions, and serve grilled andouille on the side.

A similar use for extra red beans, is to smother a burger with them. Serious.

Wild Rice and Spaghetti Sauce

A favorite in Eunice, Louisiana. Bake cooked wild rice with plum tomatoes, mushrooms, plenty of butter and seasonings for 90 minutes, whilst you go to church.

When you return, poach some eggs, place on rice and top with last night's spaghetti sauce. Keep in oven for a further 10-15 minutes and serve. Sounds good heh?

(Spaghetti sauce is ground beef flavored with trinity (see p. 24), tomato juice, tomato purée, and seasonings).

Omelettes

If you ever hold a large brunch or open a restaurant, be very careful about chalking the word 'omelette' up on the menu board. I repeatedly gave myself heart tremors by masochistically pretending I could cook them. I usually made the attempt when I thought business would be slack. But they always became my Sunday nightmare. They are certainly a nightmare, but can also be glorious. At home, I suggest you obtain yourself a pan purely for omelette cooking and once happy with it, use it for nothing else. If you catch Biff blackening his freshly caught sheepshead in it, smack him.

When executed properly, omelettes will definitely make sure the first round of Sunday drinks is not on you. I don't think there is any real need to flip. An opened-faced omelette looks better, tastes better, and is by far easier to accomplish. Master the egg mixture first, then play around with the ingredients. Add whatever you fancy, go crazy, be wild, get out of hand, how about sea urchins? Just remember, some ingredients may need pre-cooking to lose some grease or juice which you don't want leaking out of the omelette. You may also want to change flavors and textures this way. The major ingredient is confidence in your own ability.

Basic method for two omelettes

5 eggs
½ tsp sea salt

1-2 tbl double cream
½ tsp coarse-ground black pepper

Beat the egg whites for a few minutes, until they hold the odd little point. Try saying 'The Saints should never have traded Hebert'. Beat the yolks together for a few minutes, then add the cream and mix but not beat.

Mix egg mixtures, then pour into your buttered omelette pan. Cook slowly, keep checking edges, but don't 'play' with them. They are ready for the filling when the bottom is brown, or if you want to flip or finish under the broiler (grill).

Eggs Barathea

Gambling is a sorry vice. I sometimes lose money on the horses. Sad? Yes, I agree. However, last year I won a few cents on a horse named Barathea, I forget which race. The jockey was Mr Lanfranco Dettori, a fine equestrian. To commemorate this great event I invented this dish.

Eggs Barathea is grilled sausage patties on English muffins, sitting in a pool of Sauce Piquante and topped with poached eggs, butterflied shrimp, and Hollandaise sauce. I was surprised at their appeal, I was just thanking Frankie. Although it did make me realize, as I ruined more poached eggs, that the life of a jockey is just like a cook's – success depends upon timing.

8 eggs
8 tomato rounds, dusted in cornmeal
8 sausages
4 English muffins, toasted

8 shrimp, de-veined and butterflied
2 cups (16 fl oz/500 ml) Sauce Piquante (p. 46)
1 cup (8 fl oz/250 ml) Hollandaise sauce (p. 195)

SERVES 4

Poach the eggs. To make sausage patties, peel the casings off your favorite sausages. Mash the meats together and season with cayenne, garlic salt, soy sauce, and maybe flour and eggs if they will not form into patties. Grill the patties, slowly. In a sauté pan, quickly cook the outsides of the tomatoes then remove, add Sauce Piquante and shrimp, and bring to simmer.

Build the dish in the following order: Sauce Piquante, muffin, tomato, sausage patty, egg, shrimp, Hollandaise sauce. No need for garnish. Enjoy.

Salmon Melt

Another fishy sandwich. Melts are an excellent concept to the many folk who have only experienced American food on this side of The Pond. The first time a melt was made for me, it was by a girl named Amy, from Scarsdale, N.Y. Despite having been aware of them for years, I was bemused. The sandwich is made as normal, but not cut. You then butter the outside of the sandwich. Weird huh? Then you pan-fry it or grill it on a griddle. It produces the best of sandwiches. I used salmon at brunch, but of course tuna is the common filler for melts.

8 oz/250 g salmon
½ cup (4 fl oz/125 ml) water
¼ cup (2 fl oz/50 ml) white wine vinegar
1 lemon, juice squeezed
4 scallions (spring onions)
1 tsp garlic salt
1 tsp coarse-ground black pepper

½ cup (4 fl oz/125 ml) mayonnaise
1 stalk celery, chopped small
4 slices bread
1 cup (10 oz/250 g) Cheddar cheese, grated
6 tbl (3 oz/75 g) softened butter
1 tbl parsley, finely chopped

SERVES 2

Poach the salmon in a little water, white wine vinegar, and lemon juice. Don't overcook. Leave to cool. Flake salmon into a mixing bowl, then combine with all ingredients except bread, cheese, parsley, and butter.

Layer two slices of bread with half the cheese, top each with salmon mix, cover with rest of cheese and add the other slice. Butter both sides, no need to tell you the butter needs to be real soft, huh? Sprinkle parsley over each side. Press in to stick. Heat butter in pan, cook both sides of sandwich twice or until you can see the cheese melting. Be careful when turning, use both hands. Fried apples are a neat garnish with Melts, fry them with a little sugar.

Elizabet's Eggs

The lady who opened Kenny's with me is called Liz. Everyone knew Liz. The 'front of house' was her domain. Presided over with a sublime Chimera-like exuberance. Perfection in an era of casual convenience.

This dish was not named after her. It is a bastard form of a dish served at the Commander's Palace in New Orleans. It is sort of a fancy version of Eggs Benedict, giving you a further example of how to play with and adapt existing dishes.

For Eggs Elizabet, the bacon or ham sits on top of deep-fried eggplant rounds (called 'guinea squash' in the Low Country). No muffins, and instead of plain Hollandaise we add fresh diced tomatoes to the sauce, making it a Choron sauce.

In my first draft of the manuscript I included a derisory comment on how French cooking always dresses up sauces with fancy names. Then I discovered a Chef named Choron, who presided over the Restaurant Voisin in Paris – famous for its cellar, for its famous customers, like Zola and Daudet, and for Chef Choron. So we have Choron Sauce

8 rounds of eggplant, peeled
2 eggs, beaten
1 cup (8 fl oz/250 ml) milk

1 tsp garlic salt
1 tsp black pepper
1 cup (5 oz/125 g) breadcrumbs

Dip the eggplant in the eggs mixed with the milk, then roll in seasoned breadcrumbs. Deep or shallow fry until crispy. Set aside, keep warm.

2 cups (16 fl oz/500 ml) Sauce Piquante (p. 46)
8 slices ham, grilled with a dash of soy and hot sauce
8 eggs, poached

2 medium tomatoes, cored and diced, briefly sautéed in butter
1 cup (8 fl oz/250 ml) Hollandaise sauce (p. 195)

SERVES 4

Top each eggplant with ham, then poached egg, smother in Sauce Piquante. Combine the tomatoes and Hollandaise sauce to make Choron Sauce. Coat the dish in Choron Sauce.

Eggs Royal Street

This is a fancy scrambled egg dish. Apparently there is a dish somewhere else with the same name, I have never come across it or discovered what it is. I just ran out of names from the French Quarter to call my dishes after. Sorry if I upset anyone.

8 large eggs
2 tsp sea salt
2 tsp coarse-ground black pepper
2 scallions (spring onions), chopped
1 small red jalapeño, finely chopped
5 tbl (2¹/₂ oz/60 g) butter

4 oz/125 g small shrimp
6 oz/175 g smoked salmon
4 tbl cognac
1tbl black caviar (real or mock)
4 lettuces, leaves tossed and dressed

SERVES 4

Beat the eggs with the sea salt and black pepper. Sauté the scallions and jalapeño in butter. Add shrimp, fold in eggs, cook fast. Just before ready add salmon, cognac and caviar. Take off heat, leave a few minutes, fold twice and serve. Garnish with dressed lettuce leaves.

Ham and Egg Sandwich

I know where I first saw this idea. It was at Jeanna's Courthouse Grocery & Deli on Whitehead in Key West, Florida. It is opposite The Green Parrot, the second-best bar in the world. The sandwich is a ham omelette liberally sprinkled with jalapeños and served between two toasted slices of sweet Cuban bread. OOH!

Smoked Salmon 'B.L.T.'

This is one of my more regal brunch dishes, consequently it can be a real bitch to put together. But it is well worth the effort, if only for the compliments expressed by everyone enjoying them. Smoked salmon replaces the bacon in the regular B.L.T.

Scrambled eggs mixed with orange caviar – salmon roe – gives a groovy, colorful touch, especially if you garnish with mock or real caviar and snipped chives.

I smoked my own salmon – it is infinitely better than store bought products, and nothing like it! You may wish to think about smoking, it will add a whole new dimension to your cooking.

4 eggs
1 tsp sea salt
1 tsp cayenne
1 tbl salmon or cod roe
Smoked salmon slices (as much as you can
   afford or want)

6 tbl (3 oz/75 g) butter
Oakleaf lettuce leaves, tossed and dressed
4 bagels, toasted
4 slices beefsteak tomato
1 tbl snipped chives
Black caviar/roe

Easy to work out. Scramble the eggs with sea salt, cayenne and salmon or pink cod roe, in butter.

Roast Eggplant Sandwich

Roast an eggplant for 20 minutes, slice, then when needed sauté in butter and soy sauce. Assemble sandwich in a toasted baguette, with a layer of Creole mustard (coarsely ground), ripe beefsteak tomatoes, watercress, and a sharp grated cheese.

If you feel foolish serving a sandwich for brunch, despite what I feel is the most informal of all meals, assemble the above as a salad and top with a well-drained poached egg or get funky and use poached quail eggs, slicing them just before serving, allowing the yolk to dribble out.

Eggs Nouvelle Orleans

Occasionally, I attempted to move away from the simple style of brunch cooking and tried to be a little more adventurous. My experiments usually failed and had me rushing back to familiar ground. This dish of shirred eggs, baked without shells, was one which actually worked. Damn thing never sold though.

5 tbl (2½ oz/60 g butter
1 tbl plain flour
2 tbl double cream
1 tsp sea salt
1 tsp coarse-ground black pepper
pinch of nutmeg

1 tbl cognac
3 cups (1 lb/450 g) crabmeat
4 eggs
1 cup (5 oz/125 g) tasso, sautéed until real crisp
3 scallions (spring onions), chopped small

Combine butter and flour in a saucepan to make a white roux, moisten with cream, add seasoning and cognac. Mix fast. Take off heat and blend in crabmeat. Portion into 4 large ramekins, or whatever serving dish will survive the oven. Top each ramekin with an egg, sprinkle with tasso and scallions. Bake in a preheated 400°F/200°C/gas mark 6, until the egg is set. About 7 minutes. You may wish to finish off the dish with a sauce such as Bordelaise - butter, olive oil and garlic.

One-Eyed Jack

I just have to tell you about the One-Eyed Jack before I close the brunch section.

Cut a loaf real thick, 2 ins/5 cm slices are good. Make a hole in the middle. Eat the middle. Butter each side and fry in a pan. Pop an egg in the hole.

The next bit is up to you. Either broil, bake or try and be clever and flip it over. Serve with link sausage. Anyways great 'eggy' bread.

Two other well-known New Orleans brunch dishes are Eggs Sardou, invented at Antoine's, popularized at Brennans – creamed spinach and artichokes – and Eggs Hussarde – bacon, tomato, Bordelaise sauce. I never enjoyed either. But they are nonetheless institutions in the Big Easy. You may wish to try them.

DESSERT

I reckon after a full Cajun-Creole dinner there will be little room left for dessert. Personally I'm not big on dessert. I have given in, however, and added a few of my successes.

Peach Ice Cream

To really finish the meal off, serve dessert with your own ice cream. Trust me, you do not need a machine.

1 lb/450 g peaches, blended until smooth (or whatever fruits you fancy)

2½ cups (1 pint/600 ml) double cream
1 cup (5 oz/125 g) icing sugar, sifted

Beat cream and sugar together until peaks form. Fold in peach purée. Pour into a deep bowl, cover with foil, and freeze until firm. Beat small batches at a time in a large bowl, until the whole mixture is smooth. Return to pan and freeze overnight. Enjoy.

Brownie Bottom Pie

This is the ultimate Brownie recipe. My presentation makes for a great visual display. Use fresh fruit of contrasting colors to garnish along with 'dessert parsley' – shaved chocolate.

3 cups (1 lb 5 oz/450 g) brown sugar
1 cup (10 oz/250 g) butter
3 eggs
1 tbl instant coffee, dissolved in 1 tbl water
4 oz/100 g dark chocolate, melted
1 ½ cups (8 oz/200 g) plain flour
Pinch of salt

1 cup (5 oz/125 g) pecans, coarsely chopped
1 cup (8 fl oz/250 ml) whipped cream
2 tbl honey
½ cup (4 fl oz/125 ml) chocolate syrup
Fresh fruit to garnish
Chocolate shavings to garnish

Cream together sugar and butter, add eggs one at a time, beating well each time. Then mix in coffee and chocolate. Fold in flour and salt and finally nuts. Spoon into a greased Swiss roll tin, 9 in x 12 in x 1.5 in/22.5 cm x 30 cm x 4 cm, preferably lined with non-stick baking paper. This allows for easier removal and for individual wrapping, if they are not to be eaten straight away.

Pre-heat oven to 350°F/180°C/gas mark 4 and bake for 25 minutes. When they leave the oven the brownies should still be a little soft to the touch, with a crust, this will mean the finished product is slightly chewy, which is what we want. Let cool and cut into squares.

To assemble your 'pie,' cut each brownie in half. Top one half with honey-whipped cream, place the other half on top, place more cream on it. Pour chocolate syrup or melted chocolate over it all. Garnish with fresh fruit and chocolate shavings.

My Black 'n' Blue Berry Cobbler

Why do all the best names for dessert come from the South?

3 cups (1 lb/450 g) fresh blueberries   *2 tbl plain flour*
1 cup (8 oz/250 g) sugar   *2 tbl brandy*
1 tsp lemon juice

Combine all the above in a bowl. Refrigerate until required.

2 eggs, beaten   *1 cup (5 oz/125 g) plain flour*
4 tbl (2 oz/50 g) butter, melted   *2 tsp baking powder*
4 tbl sugar   *pinch of salt*

Mix eggs, butter and sugar together. Sift together flour and baking powder. Add salt. Slowly sift into egg mix.

Place berries in a baking dish, haphazardly cover with the dough, dot with butter and bake for 30 minutes at 375°F/190°C/gas mark 5. Serve straight from the oven with pouring cream and a fresh fruit garnish.

Peanut Butter Cookies

½ cup (5 oz/125 g) butter or shortening
   (cooking fat)
½ cup (2½ oz/60 g) dark brown sugar
½ cup (2½ oz/60 g) light brown sugar
½ tsp salt
½ tsp bicarbonate of soda

1¼ cups (6½ oz/165 g) plain flour
1 cup (5 oz/125 g) crunchy peanut butter
1 tsp vanilla essence
1 egg
4 tbl crushed peanuts to garnish
4 tbl honey-whipped cream

Beat together the butter or shortening with the dark brown sugar and the light brown sugar. Sift together half a teaspoon each of salt and baking soda with the flour. Beat together the crunchy peanut butter, vanilla essence, and one egg. Add to sugar mix then blend in flour. Make into a dough, then roll it out and cut it into your favorite cookie shape. Place on a greased baking tray and bake in a pre-heated oven at 375°F/190°C/gas mark 5 for 10 minutes. Serve with vanilla ice cream.

To make into a Peanut Butter Pie, add a can of evaporated milk, ½ cup (4 fl oz/125 ml) corn syrup, and two more eggs, pour into a pie crust and bake. Serve topped with crushed peanuts and honey-whipped cream. (Urgh!)

Cheesecake

Cheesecakes to me are easy. I find it surprising that they posed me few problems, as they really do require proper attention. There are two basic types of cheesecake, the dense New York style or the airier, ricotta cheese Italian rendition.

Today though, all sorts are being invented, for example my crab cheesecake (p. 111).

I attempted funky flavors and textures, but I invariably ended up back at a basic few – lemon, chocolate, banana, and strawberry. The one big seller

of all time was expensive to make but worth it, Amaretto cheesecake. It stimulated booze sales too.

Lemon Cheesecake

Biscuit base

1 1/4 cups (6 1/2 oz/165 g) graham crackers or
   digestive biscuits, crushed
1 tbl brown sugar

1 tsp cinnamon
3 tbl (1 1/2 oz/40 g) melted butter

Mix together, press into greased 8 in/20 cm springform tin. Bake for 5-10 minutes.

3 cups (1 lb/450 g) Cream cheese
1 cup (5 oz/125 g) sugar
3 eggs
3 lemons, juice squeezed and zest grated

1 cup (8 fl oz/250 ml) sour cream
2 tsp cornflour
1/2 tsp vanilla essence

In a large bowl, break down cheese and combine with sugar. Beat in eggs, lemon juice and zest, vanilla essence, and cornflour. Stir in sour cream, mix well pour over base. Bake in a pre-heated 350°F/180°C/gas mark 4 oven for 60 minutes, you could use a bain-marie. Turn off oven and leave the cheesecake alone for 60 minutes with the door slightly open.

Vermont Pumpkin Cheesecake

The key here is the pumpkin pie spice mix, which consists of equal quantities of mace, allspice, nutmeg, ginger, and cinnamon. Make as for the Lemon Cheesecake above, but add the spice mix, a can of pumpkin, substitute half a cup of double cream for the sour cream and substitute

brown for the white sugar. The pie will be deeper so obviously use a bigger pan.

Serve with Butterscotch Sauce: heat 1 cup sugar, $^1/_2$ cup corn syrup, and 4 tbl (2 oz/50 g) butter together. As soon as you reach a caramel color, add $^1/_2$ cup (4 fl oz/125 ml) double cream and a dash of bourbon. Serve straight away.

Lafayette Pecan Pie

Pecan pie is not difficult at all to make. And it annoys me when I see so many restaurants buying it in. Can they cook at all? Should we maybe rename these joints, 'convenience stores with service'? At Kenny's, we always aimed to use corn syrup in our pecan pies, but this was not always possible. Nonetheless, regular golden syrup is usually fine.

Easy Pastry Crust

1 $^1/_4$ cups (6 $^1/_2$ oz/165 g) plain flour
2 tsp icing sugar
pinch salt

$^1/_2$ cup (5 oz/125 g) shortening (margarine) or melted butter
2 tbl cold water

Sift flour, sugar, and salt together. Add shortening and water. Form into a ball. Grease an 8 in/20 cm fluted, loose-bottomed pie dish. Push the crust into place. Refrigerate. Do not bake 'blind.'

4 tbl (2 oz/50 g) melted butter, slightly cooled
3 eggs
pinch salt
$^1/_2$ cup (2 $^1/_2$ oz/60 g) brown sugar

1 tbl golden syrup or dark corn syrup
$^1/_2$ tsp vanilla essence
1 cup (5 oz/125 g) pecan halves

In a large bowl, beat eggs, mix in rest of ingredients, combine well. Pour into pie crust - gently. Pre-heat oven to 350°F/180°C/gas mark 4. Bake for 30 minutes or until filling is set. It may rise high, but don't worry - it will sort itself out. Turn off oven, open door and leave it inside for 15 minutes. Nice smell, huh?

Divide the pie into portions and serve with vanilla ice cream or honey-whipped cream and garnish with fresh fruit.

Sweet Potato Pecan Pie

This was difficult to sell, but it is popular in Louisiana and smells great even to me. You can either top a regular pecan pie with a flavored mash of sweet potatoes and then bake. Or blend in the potatoes to the pecan mix and bake. Both work, and will surprise your guests. Just make sure you add nutmeg and cinnamon to the potatoes when you mash them.

Mom's Apple Pie

The pie comes out better if one third of the cooking fat is lard.

Pastry dough

3¹/₂ cups (18 oz/500 g) plain flour
2 tbl icing sugar
¹/₂ tsp salt

1 cup (10 oz/250 g) shortening (margarine) cut
into pieces
1 egg yolk mixed with 3 tbl cold water

Mix flour, sugar, and salt in a large bowl, add shortening, and blend in with fingers until mixture resembles fine breadcrumbs. Bind together with egg-and-water mixture. Knead on floured surface with fingertips, until a smooth ball is formed. Cover in clingfilm. Rest in fridge for at least one hour.

Pie filling

3 lb/1 ½ kg cooking apples
Sugar to taste

1 tbl cinnamon
1 egg, beaten with 4 tbls milk

Partly stew apples in water. Cool. I find you will be able to stuff more apple in the pie by part-stewing. Add sugar to taste. Line individual greased pie tins with pastry, cut out rounds for lids. Fill with cooled apples, add a little cinnamon. Wet edges of crust with water, put on lid, seal well by crimping. Glaze with egg-and-milk wash and sprinkle top with sugar.

Pre-heat oven to 400°F/200°C/gas mark 6, bake for 10 minutes. Lower temperature to 350°F/180°C/gas mark 4, then bake for a further 30 minutes max.

In the South 'fry pies' are big news. Make as above, but deep-fry instead of bake. Favorite fillers are banana, blueberry and apple.

Key Lime Pie

Biscuit base as for cheesecake (p. 225)
2 juicy limes, juice and grated zest

2 eggs
1 can of sweetened condensed milk

Press the base into a greased pie dish. Combine the limes, eggs, and condensed milk and pour onto pie crust. Bake at 350°F/180°C/gas mark 4 for 30 minutes. Don't let the top crack (maybe bake in bain marie?). This is a small version of the classic pie. It is rich, so think about it. You may wish to be traditional and bake it with a meringue topping or alternatively, serve it with whipped cream. I prefer the pie plain and small, just garnished with a lime wheel - twisted - and icing sugar. It is a refreshing way to end a big, flavor-packed meal.

Strawberry Shortcake

This is a really popular dessert all over the States. Whenever we posted it on the menu board, the S.S. would walk out the door. Being a restaurant, we had to make the shortcake ourselves, which requires semolina in the mix. It is a biscuit type of pastry. I suggest you go to the store and buy the shortcake. Much easier. If you are a dessert freak, buy Marjorie Kinnan Rawling's *Cross Creek Cooking*, published in 1942, to see how to prepare it properly.

Make a strawberry sauce, maybe with canned or frozen strawberries, liquor, and cream. Top one split shortcake with whipped cream, add fresh strawberries to the dish, and smother with sauce. Garnish with mint leaves and sieved icing sugar.

Mint Julep Pound Cake

This a plain cake, which derives its name from the original 1747 recipe – one pound each of flour, butter, eggs, and sugar. The recipe these days has become a little more refined. I enjoy mint julep flavorings in many dishes, here they are wonderfully highlighted.

3 cups (1 lb/450 g) plain flour
1 1/2 tsp baking powder
1/2 tsp salt
1 cup (10 oz/250 g) butter, softened
3 cups (1 lb/450 g) sugar

5 large eggs
1/2 cup (4 fl oz/125 ml) double cream
1 tsp mint extract, if you make this yourself you
*   will need more.*
3 tbl bourbon whiskey

Sift together the flour, baking powder, and salt. Cream the butter and sugar. Add eggs and mix until the batter resembles mayonnaise. Gradually mix in flour, then the cream. Finally add the mint and bourbon. Pre-heat oven to 300°F/150°C/gas mark 2. Pour batter into a 10 in/25 cm lightly greased cake tin. Only fill the tin half to two-thirds. Bake in the middle of the oven for 90 to 110 minutes or until the cake is springy. Cool for 20 minutes and remove from the tin.

Mile High Ice Cream Pie

Some say Marco Polo launched the idea for ice cream. I like to think the Latin alternative is the truth. They will have it that Montezuma, the Aztec Emperor, had servants pour liquid chocolate onto the mountain snows and then had the resulting mix rushed back to him. Prepare this dessert for someone special, otherwise you may become a little despondent with humanity. The motivation behind convincing myself to make it.

(The oven needs to be very hot, otherwise you will have the gastronomic equivalent of Pharos Lighthouse).

3 1 pint/600 ml cartons of ice cream - red, white and brown e.g., cherry, vanilla, chocolate
Biscuit base as for cheesecake (p. 225)
6 egg whites
½ cup (2½ oz/60 g) castor sugar
½ tsp vanilla essence
1 big pinch cream of tartar

Layer the ice cream in an 8 in/20 cm plastic bowl, leave 1in/2.5 cm at the top. Place in freezer. Make the biscuit base. Place it over the ice cream and return to the freezer. Leave until tomorrow.

The next day make a meringue with the egg whites, castor sugar, vanilla essence, and a big pinch of tartar, or as you normally do.

Pre-heat the oven to at least 450°F/230°C/gas mark 8.

Dip the ice cream bowl in warm water to loosen it. (Keep the base out!) Remove bowl and turn onto a ovenproof plate, larger than 8 in/20 cm. Smother the ice cream with meringue. Place in oven. As soon as the meringue has browned, 2-3 minutes, remove. Freeze straight away. Have a drink.

To make a whole pie can be expensive, especially if Ben & Jerry's is your favorite ice cream. So think of making individual versions; with a little imagination it will not be difficult.

Delta Mud Pie

Make a biscuit base in a springform tin. Bring your favorite ice cream to a soft state, but do not let it melt. Maybe mix two together. Press ice cream into the tin, making sure the base is fully covered. You may wish to top the pie with nuts or shaved chocolate. Freeze until firm. Cut the pie into portions and smother in hot chocolate sauce. Serve it fast, we don't want it too muddy!

I presume you can make hot chocolate sauce. You melt chocolate over a double boiler with double cream, and keep it warm. Some folk simmer cocoa with butter and water, adding sugar and a liqueur for flavor, but this is getting a little too complicated in my view.

Fried Ice Cream

2 cups (10 oz/250 g) graham crackers or
  digestive biscuits
4 tbl sugar
1 cup (5 oz/125 g) pecans, finely chopped or
  ground
2 eggs, beaten

2 cups (16 fl oz/500 ml) vanilla ice cream,
  softened
1 cup (8 fl oz/250 ml) milk
About 1 cup (8 fl oz/250 ml) maple or golden
  syrup to serve

This is wild. Crush graham crackers or digestive biscuits with sugar and pecans.

Use an ice-cream scoop to form the ice cream into balls. Re-freeze.

Make an egg-milk batter. Roll ice cream in batter then in crumbs, repeat. Deep fry in fresh oil at 350°F/180°C until crumbs brown. Smother in syrup and serve immediately.

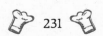

Pralines

PRAH-leens are flat, round nut candies. They are another delicacy peculiar to the Crescent City. Today they come in a multitude of flavors. The original however, is sugar, butter, and vanilla, with pecans. The best store to find them, is the 65-year-old Aunt Sally's in the French Market. Corn syrup can be found in specialty shops, but if it not available use half the quantity of liquid glucose – available from pharmacists. Both have the effect of stopping the sugar from crystallizing.

2 cups (10 oz/250 g) granulated sugar
1 cup (5 oz/125 g) brown sugar
½ cup (2½ oz/60 g) unsalted butter

2 tbl light corn syrup or 1 tbl liquid glucose
3 cups (12 oz/350 g) pecans
2 tsp vanilla essence

You need to work FAST and have all ingredients prepared. Non-stick baking paper or a marble slab, as at Aunt Sally's, will be required. Make sure they are ready before cooking.

Combine all the ingredients in a heavy-based saucepan, preferably of untinned copper. Bring to the boil, and boil steadily for as long as it takes for the mix to become soft and manageable; in New Orleans they call this the 'soft ball stage.' Take off heat and drop by tablespoons onto non-stick baking paper. Let cool and eat.

Pralines are bit of a science, many folk call for candy thermometers and exact temperatures. If you are worried about when the mixture is ready, drop a little into bowl of cold water, if it forms a ball, you're okay.

N'Awlins Bread Pudding
with Whiskey Sauce

3¹/₂ cups (1¹/₂ pints/875 ml) milk
4 thick slices stale bread or half a small baguette
   one or two days' old.
¹/₃ cup (2 oz/50 g) brown sugar
2 eggs, beaten
1 cup (5 oz/125 g) raisins
¹/₂ cup (2¹/₂ oz/60 g) hazelnuts

5 tbl (2¹/₂ oz/60 g) melted butter, cooled
1 tbl baking powder
¹/₂ tsp cinnamon
¹/₄ tsp vanilla essence
4 squares or so of grated dark chocolate
¹/₂ tsp grated nutmeg

In a large bowl soak bread in milk. Go for coffee. Mix all ingredients into the bread, except half chocolate and nutmeg.

Pour mixture into greased baking dish, sprinkle nutmeg and chocolate over the top.

Pre-heat oven to 350°F/180°C/gas mark 4 and bake for 60 minutes or until set.

Whiskey sauce

4 tbl (2 oz/50 g) butter
4 tbl sugar
4 tbl double cream

Juice of 1 orange
¹/₂ cup (4 fl oz/125 ml) whiskey

It is up to you how much you make of it but here is a basic recipe. Melt the butter in a pan, add sugar. Cook for 2-3 minutes add double cream and a little orange juice, blend in. Add all the whiskey you like. As soon as the sauce begins to stick it should be ready. You may want to taste first! Smother the bread pudding in sauce and garnish with icing sugar. Enjoy.

LAGNIAPPE

Lagniappe

Lagniappe is a term used by the Creoles of New Orleans, which means 'a little *extra*' or as we would say 'a baker's dozen.' It comes from the Spanish word for gift 'la napa.'

Here is a quotation from *Life on the Mississippi* by Mark Twain, published in 1883.

'We picked up one *excellent* word — a word worth traveling to New Orleans to get; a nice, limber, expressive, handy, word — 'Lagniappe'. They pronounce it lanny-yap.. It is something thrown in, gratis, for good measure...'F'rth lagniappe, sah...'.

Now for my lagniappe:

Don't stand up in a canoe.
If you spill oil, cover it in salt, and sweep up.
Never go for a pee after chopping chiles.
Don't eat 'cooter,' it's box turtle.
Abdominal obesity, your beer gut, is caused by the devil in your brain telling you to have those extra three drinks.
Foresee your guests' needs and desires.
In Japanese, oyster is 'kaki.'
Never refrigerate tomatoes; cold will kill the flavor. For maximum flavor, eat at room temperature.
Storing mushrooms in the same fridge as other food, will also speed up their fungal qualities.
You can always tell the female blue crab by her painted fingernails – the femme fatale of the crustacean world.
Don't ask your waitress from Tennessee to go buy smoking chips she may return with BBQ-flavored Pringles.
If you come across datura in a Native American restaurant – pass. It is a crazy violent hallucinogen, derived from the thorn apple.

'Nekkid' in the South isn't just naked, it means you are naked fixin' to do something.

'Brushwood Shrimp' are grasshoppers in Chinese.

Companies are not good at managing people, only at making money.

Susan Spicer is the cutest chef in New Orleans.

Think when you drink (and drive).

Okay that's your lot folks, for the time being.

I hope you enjoyed reading about my ideas on the world of food, my paean to the Muse Casterea.

With many regrets I spent twelve years in the restaurants of London. But it was one hell of a learning curve. (T.L.C.)

I think food, particularly when it is produced and executed properly, represents the soul of our existence. Even if mine is covered in scar tissue.

Many folk 'dis' food. That it is their problem. For them 'il pleure dans mon coeur comme il pleut sur la ville.'

When those of us who do care, bother to prepare food with proper attention, it is there to make our lives better. Enjoy.

For now, so long.

Amitiés gourmandes

KENNY.
FALL '95

Remember – LOVE IS LIKE A CHEF FROM HELL.

A quick guide to my cooking terms and ingredients

Andouille - (an-doo-eey) a smoked spicy sausage. Spanish chorizo or Polish kielbasa can be substituted.

Beignets - fluffy deep-fried fritters.

Bisquits - puffy leavened bread similar to soda bread. Served at dinner.

Blackening - a style of cooking that originated in the kitchens of Chef Paul Prudhomme in 1980. You coat fish or meat in herbs and spices, then sear it in a white-hot skillet. This seals the outer crust, allowing all the juices to remain on the inside.

Buttermilk - the sour liquid containing a little butterfat, left after the making of butter.

Chicken - the domesticated Red Jungle fowl from India. Please buy the best you can find. It will be worth it.

Chiles - I generally use Jalapeños or Scotch Bonnets. I suggest you experiment and settle on one you are happy with. Remember to respect them and prepare them properly. They can ruin a guests evening if you take short cuts. When I discuss diced chile peppers, I mean they should be topped, cut in half, de-seeded and de-veined. This is important.

Cobbler - a deep-dish pie with a thick crust and fruit filling.

Coddle - to cook just below boiling point.

Cornbread - a light bread made from cornmeal.

Cornmeal - a usually yellow meal ground from dried maize.

Crab - Blue crabs are my favorite, with their bluey-green shell. Unfortunately we have to make do wth our own indigenous Brown Crab.

Crawfish - a tiny freshwater version of the Rock Lobster.

Creole Sauce - a base for many dishes, such as Jambalaya. The main ingredients are tomatoes and trinity with strong seasonings.

Cup - Americans measure lots of ingredients in cups, including butter and even vegetables. A standard American cup holds 8 fl oz/250 ml of liquid, but because it is a volume measure, solids will measure differently, depending on how heavy they are. A rule of thumb is that a cup of most powdery solids, such as flour and icing sugar, will weigh 5 oz/125 g. Most standard measuring cups that are sold nowadays are American cup measures, made in the Far East in the size which fits the biggest market. Choose one you are happy with and use it for cooking with. If you start cooking with cups it will soon become easy for you. Much quicker than weighing and measuring, especially for such items as sugar and flour.

Debris - the remains in a roasting tray after cooking, such as roast beef debris. Ideal for gravies or po' boys.

Eggplant - Aubergine.

Eggs - all eggs are English size 2.

En Papillote - baking in a paper bag.

Etouffée - a method of cooking, where your favorite food is smothered in a blanket of chopped vegetables and slowly cooked down.

Filé - a flavoring agent made from ground sassafras (a member of the laurel family) leaves.

Fish:

Catfish - a freshwater, spiny, scaleless fish. Very popular in the South. Farmed catfish taste like wild trout.

Flounder - not Sole. Same family as Halibut.

Mahi Mahi - Dolphin fish, NOT the mammal. Excellent. Lean and sweet.

Permit - A member of the Jack family. The Permit is a highly sought after fish by game anglers. It is part of the Grand Slam, - where one attempts to catch a Snook, Permit, Tarpon and Bone Fish in the same day. (I'm still trying!)

Pompano - a member of the Jack family, revered in New Orleans.

Trout - please don't bother with farmed trout (same with Salmon). In L.A. the Gulf Speckled Trout, of the Weakflsh family is popular.

Fricassée - browned meats covered in gravy and cooked down. Today the term almost exclusively refers to poultry in a white sauce.

'Gator - El Lagarto. The alligator is no longer protected and there is even a burgeoning 'gator farming industry. The meat is best from the tail and is similar to pork with a mild fishy flavor.

Groundnut Oil - Peanut oil. Used for all my deep, and most of my shallow frying.

Gumbo - a thick hearty stew.

Ham Hock - knuckle of pork.

Hoppin' John - a cooked dish of black eye peas, ham and rice.

Hot Sauce - a fermented condiment made from chile peppers and vinegar.

Hush Puppies - small cornmeal fritters, designed to shut up the dogs, but nowadays more often found beside Fried Catfish.

Jambalaya - a highly seasoned rice dish, usually including tomatoes, ham and shrimp.

Liquid smoke - a condiment made from the condensation that collects in a smoke house. Used the same way as a hot sauce it is readily available at larger supermarkets.

Mirliton - a vegetable similar to a pale green squash.

Molasses - sweet brown syrup from sugar cane or sorghum.

Muffuletta - a discus shaped sandwich packed with olive salad, cheeses and hams.

Okra - a much-maligned tropical vegetable pod which originates from Africa.

Oyster Shooter - a cocktail made with Cajun Vodka, Bloody Mary mix and an oyster.

Pecans - a nut from the American Hickory tree.

Po-Boy - a standard New Orleans sandwich made in a baguette.

Pralines - a candy made wlth brown sugar, milk and pecans.

Ramekin - a small dish used for baking and/or serving individual portions.

Roux - a sauce made up of equal parts of oil and flour, cooked to a dark color. An essential element in many Louisiana dishes.

Sauce Piquant - a spicy tomato sauce with a roux and usually red wine.

Shrimp - shrimp is an all encompassing term for members of the crustacean order Decapoda (ten legged). It includes prawns but not lobsters. It is sensible to buy them frozen, as they spoil easy. I generally use the size 21-25. This means you will receive between 21 and 25 per pound.

"Shucked" - when oysters are opened or corn cobs removed from their husks.

Soft Shell Crabs - all crustaceans moult. The blue crab is highly prized in this condition. The whole creature is eaten.

Soy Sauce - not often thought of as being used in Southern cooking. But I feel the strong, slightly salty flavor of fermented soy beans works well.

Sweet Potatoes - a semantic nightmare. In Louisiana the yam is a strain of sweet potato and often the names are interchanged.

Tasso - spicy smoked ham from Louisiana, used mainly in flavoring. There is a recipe for making it at home on p. 149 but you can substitute any good-quality smoked ham.

Tenths - I cut a chicken up into ten pieces, discarding the back and wingtips. Remove the wings, cut the legs off and then cut them in two, and cut the breast into four. Easy.

Tomatoes - please take the time to source a serious supplier. Vine ripened are best.

Trinity - equal parts of chopped onion, celery, and bell pepper (green or red depending on the dish).

V-8 juice - when required, nothing else will do. NOTHING! It is tomato and vegetable juice made by Campbells.

Any problems – drop me a line.

Bibliography

Some books I enjoy cooking from; they are:

NEW NEW ORLEANS COOKING, Emeril Lagasse, William Morrow, 1993

SPOONBREAD AND STRAWBERRY WINE, Norma Darden, Fawcett, 1978

THE MAKING OF A COOK, Madeleine Kamman, Atheneum, 1971

HOW FRENCH WOMEN COOK, Madeleine Kamman, Atheneum, 1976

THE PICAYUNE CREOLE COOKBOOK, Dover Publications, 1971

FOG CITY DINER COOKBOOK, Cindy Pawclyn, Ten Speed Press, 1993

NEW AMERICAN CLASSICS, Jeremiah Tower, Harper & Row, 1986

COYOTE CAFE, Mark Miller, Ten Speed Press, 1989

ADVENTURES IN THE KITCHEN, Wolfgang Puck, Random House, 1991

FEAST OF SUNLIGHT, Norman Van Akens, Ballantyne, 1988

FARMHOUSE COOKBOOK, Susan Herrmann Loomis, Workman Publishing, 1991

BREAKFAST, LUNCH & DINNER, Bradley Ogden, Random House, 1991

COOKING WITH NATURAL FLAVORS, Edith & Sam Brown, Hawthorn, 1972

MEMORIES OF GASCONY, Pierre Koffman, Pyramid, 1990

GOOSE FAT AND GARLIC, Jeanne Strang, Kyle Cathie, 1991

CHEZ HELENE - HOUSE OF GOOD FOOD, Austin Leslie, De Simonin, 1984

CHEZ PANISSE COOKING, Paul Bertolli & Alice Waters, Random House, 1988

FRENCH COOKING, Elizabeth David, Dorling Kindersley, 1987

SPIRIT OF THE HARVEST, B. Cox & M. Jacobs, Stewart, Tabori & Chang, 1991

TRADE WINDS, Cristine Mackie, Absolut Press, 1987

CROSS CREEK COOKERY, Marjorie Kinnan Rawlings, Scribners, 1942

. . . learning from;

THE UNPREJUDICED PALATE, Angello Pellegrini, Nth Point Press, 1984

LIVING BY THE WORD, Alice Walker, Women's Press, 1988

SILENT SPRING, Rachel Carson, Penguin, 1962

AMERICAN FRIED, Calvin Trillin,Vintage, 1979

DIET FOR A NEW AMERICA, John Robbins, Stillpoint, 1987

ON FOOD & COOKING, Harold McGee, Unwin Hyman, 1984

THE WASTED OCEAN, David K. Bulloch, L&B, 1989

THE FLIGHT OF THE IGUANA, David Quammen, Anchor, 1988

EIGHT LITTLE PIGGIES, Stephen Jay Gould, Penguin, 1993

WITH BOLD KNIFE AND FORK, M.F.K. Fisher, Chatto & Windus, 1983

THE ALICE B. TOKLAS COOK BOOK, Alice B. Toklas, Brilliance, 1983

BETWEEN MEALS, A.J. Liebling, Nth Point Press, 1986

TASTE OF AMERICA, John L. Hess & Karen Hess, Penguin, 1986

THE PHILOSOPHER IN THE KITCHEN, J-A Brillat-Savarin, Penguin, 1970

THE COMPLEAT ANGLER, Izaak Walton, Everyman edition, 1993

BEAUTIFUL SWIMMERS, William Warner, Penguin, 1976

DELIGHTS & PREJUDICES, James Beard, Atheneum, 1964

INDEX